Grace Under Pressure

Grace Under Pressure
A Southern Belle in the City

Dori Bibb Cook, M.Ed.

Bibb Cook, Dori, author: Grace Under Pressure, A
Southern Belle in the City
Book design by KDP
Includes bibliographical references and index
ISBN 978-0-578-92701-5 (Pbk)
  1. Love, Life, Marriage   2. Divorce and Infertility 3.
     Transformation

"Instead of letting your hardships and failures discourage or exhaust you, let them inspire you. Let them make you even hungrier to succeed," M.O.

Contents

Preface

You are my village. You, that's right. You. Are. Apart. of. My. Village! We are about to get real intimate, so that makes you a part of my village. So it's just as much your responsibility as it is mine to care for this village. Our job is to protect this village, guide, teach, and uplift the village to be its best self. We do this by sharing the lessons learned and how we are resilient in the face of adversity. The strength and resilience of our village are not inevitable, but it is impenetrable if we are good stewards to the village. So come be in this village with music to dance, sing the melodies and embrace each other as we dance these songs in the key of our lives...

Be the Village!

This book is my declaration to the world that my purpose in life is to be a forceful soul in the village. It is my responsibility as a mother and as a sister of this village. Though deceased since 1990, my grandmother, a devotee to the village, has remained a prominent figure in my reflections and thoughts on the role I've played in the village. One of the most important legacies she left the village and me is the notion of love, community, belief in yourself, and counting it all joy. A few years ago, I went through a series of life experiences that turned my world upside down. My life didn't look the same as it had been, notwithstanding how I had imagined it would be as I started. Whether it was in love, professionally or personally, it was different, an irregular fit. I felt as though something or someone had overthrown the chessboard and lost all of my footings.

I was standing on quicksand, it seemed. By the time I arrived in Northern Virginia, all of my obstacles were manageable, but now, I was far from home, far away from family, far away from true and lifelong friends, miles away from the neighborhoods that I know and love. Just too damn far away from what I considered my center. And the penultimate of it all was this journey thus far to the DMV to the heart of Dixie. The prescription was a couple of jagged little pills that became the impetus to seasons of unbelievable strength, remarkable resilience, and uncontainable sparkle as I walked through the fire of refinement.

Much like other African American Women from the South, my marriage, child, and career are the defining moments signifying a well-rounded life, an accomplishment, badges of honor bestowed upon great women. But, of course, as a Daughter of the South, these notions were simultaneously embedded within my dreams as I continued to go on this adventure.

From my divorce five years after this significant migration to the north, I encountered hardships professionally and personally with those I chose to be in my village. I always scoffed at the retorts of "it will all work out" because sometimes my anxiety gets the best of me. No, I am not perfect by any means, and there are times when I need a cheerleader to see it through. But when you are going through, it can be challenging to hear the cheers and believe the hype. So, I took to journaling and considering how I had been prepared for these moments. What about my upbringing helped to equip me with the tools to survive and thrive? Which took me back to the days when my grandmother and I would discuss her hardships and how she overcame them. She always gave me tidbits of advice to hold dear. There were also little things like always having earrings on when you leave the house, wearing pantyhose in the right color when in a professional setting, never being afraid to be a woman. She was a firm believer that God gave women things like intuition, femininity, and the ability to love through it all. As a little girl typically sitting next to her with alert ears, I remembered when she showed me one of her pearl necklaces that she treasured and would wear to church or on nice occasions. Ms. Mary explained to me the significance of a pearl and how it resembles the process of enduring life. There will always be obstacles but what you make of it is the most critical part of the struggle.

A couple of years after arriving in Northern Virginia, as I sat in the parking lot of my apartment, it all came flooding back to my memory with one look in my rearview mirror. I was missing my earrings, and looking at the time on my car's clock, I had to find a quick resolution to this problem. A trusty second pair of pearls in my wallet will do the trick, I thought. And voila! I found them and thought of the message my grandmother handed me years ago as a young girl. First, respecting myself equals self-confidence, be sure of who I am because I was raised to be an excellent example for others in the village to trust and embrace. Secondly, I am made from a "good stock," so I can endure anything. And last but not least, count it all joy because everything in life is an opportunity to learn something new about myself and the power within me.

Introduction

I am overwhelmed by the grace and persistence of my people.

Maya Angelou

This statement by the great Maya Angelou sums up the lives of my people both near and far in this world. When I consider my people globally, regionally, and locally or on a familial level, I am reminded that a person is the summation of their interpretations of their environmental experiences. And my people have endured a lot to survive in this world. But when you consider all that we endure, one must ask themselves how do they do it? How do Black people wake up every day to carry on? These were things that my friends in undergrad and I would ponder. All while sitting on my green striped couch, Bob Marley on the stereo, close friends grinning, ki-ki-ing about how we can change the world, would set the stage for considering why this statement "perception is reality" is the key to all things.   --Lee Atwater.

When it comes to perception, African Americans are a perfect example of this notion due to the traumatization of its people for over 400 years, 40+ generations. My philosophy is the Black Woman is the mother of the earth, and her sons and daughters have experienced trauma on a cellular level, epigenetics. I have had my own family's traumatic experiences to see how a child's environment impacts their take on the world around them. Understanding how my people have developed coping mechanisms, whether healthy or unhealthy, helped shape my life journey. Later I'd learn the scientific name for this process, the transactional model of development by A. Sameroff.

Both the professional and personal realms of society have always had this same perspective of how trauma is transactional within people and generations of the same circles throughout my life. Although many areas of my life have this aspect, church, high school, adult, and professionally are/were explicitly service-oriented towards women and children.

My mother's gynecologist and my 10th-grade Biology teacher inspired me. The interest in both subjects happened to propel my learning experiences into a week-long STEM conference-specific focus. The gratification of helping others cope with trauma and its impacts on their family members became a vision set in serving women and children while encouraging healthy relationships amongst themselves and their communities.

If someone would have asked me 25 years ago, "How do I imagine my life?" My vision would not have been the journey I have traveled since moving to the nation's capital, Washington, DC. I have had some beautiful times throughout this journey, and I have had some growing to do along the way. Each time was learning to find the blessing from the lesson and realizing my strength, ability to be resilient, and the ability to shine on anyway despite the things that tried to dim my light and diminish my power. I am glad that I am still a work in progress, but I feel that I have the right mix of ME.

This realization brings me to the most recent years, which had me perched on the precipice of transition. To quell my anxiety when considering the notion of it all, I'd journal my thoughts with several glasses of Malbec while listening to Jill Scott. Then, with my favorite pen trying to map out a plan to address the stops along the way, I'd strategize my next move. One day while I was journaling, I was distracted by the clock at 3:30 pm and the acknowledgment that I have to be ready for a show at 6:30 pm—distracted by the notion of what I would wear and what jewelry I would select for the evening. Pearls are my signature jewelry. Pearls are dear to me given that I've worn them most of my life, it is the jewelry of my sisterhood, and it is a Southern Belle; a pearl is a rare stone, thus denotes a status of elegance. This evening when considering the concept of a pearl, the nacre, or the shiny stuff lining the edges of the clam, was intriguing to me. I felt encouraged to continue to contemplate this notion of the mollusk and its built-in and ready-made army. I'd typically factor in at least a 20 min buffer to accommodate any traffic jams on 295 when commuting to DC from Alexandria. So, I was already pushing into my buffer arrival time for the office. What makes the pearl a unique stone? Why would a woman associate high value and social connotations with this stone? Maybe because the pearl is one of the oldest jewels related to high society worldwide. Cleopatra is said to have crushed one and served it in a drink to Marc Antony to prove her status. Southern Belles are raised understanding the associations with pearls, and so I had several pairs. So, I picked up my trusty journal to scribble down a bit about the pearls and how they are formed.

How is this thing called nacre activated once there is an intruder or irritant to my homeostasis? And what process does this nuisance have in creating a beautiful stone coveted by humankind for centuries? Nacre is defined as a strong, resilient, and luminous substance that lines the clam and protects the muscle from harmful intruders. Suppose I consider my little world as a mollusk lined with nacre inside the clam, a layer of protection. In that case, I can pinpoint ample instances where an irritant came into my life, disrupted and unsettled my quiet environment. Every time this happened, I would have to develop my strengths, construct a resilient spirit and keep calm and carry on. I had to learn to shine in my small victories as hardships arose.

Three ties that bind; strength, resilience, and acknowledging your wins (what I like to call "Sparkle On!") is a chord of protection and transformation, unbeknownst to me sometimes, their collaboration seemingly noticing my efforts through to the end. And I realized that this happened with every scenario along my journey. As a southern belle raised in the deep south, pearls are a considerable part of my personality in that I wear them to express refinement and femininity. This concept of nacre and its protection of the mollusk speaks to my life as a Black woman and as a mother, businesswoman/mentor, and friend. The many different aspects of my life along this journey have demonstrated the power of my built-in defense mechanisms and the pearls that I display to denote my victory and triumph.

Reminiscing on situations and opportunities overcome with strength is the fuel of my dreams coming to fruition. Several historical scenarios are peppered with instances where I learned to be grateful for the legacy of my roots. My legacy is the foundation of my strength, a strategic application of my efforts, and utilization of the results to provide a balance to my life and keep me on my toes. I thank God for the foundation supplanted by my ancestors, which created a solid platform to positively impact the world around me, inspiring others to believe in themselves and teaching me to embrace my strength.

Like Dorothy in The Wiz, my story begins with a blended family with lots of love and embracing the circle of life at my grandma's house.

PART I

Strength

There's no place like home.

When I think of home

I think of a place where there's love overflowing

I wish I was home

I wish I was back there with the things I been knowing

Wind that makes the tall trees bend into leaning

Suddenly the snowflakes that fall have a meaning

Sprinklin' the scene makes it all clean

Maybe there's a chance for me to go back

Now that I have some direction

It would sure be nice to be back home

My first address to note was in the inconspicuously sleepy southern city of Montgomery, Alabama. West Patton Avenue is a long bustling street (at least that's how I remember it) in the Ridgecrest neighborhood with Black families in every direction as far as you can see. Although W. Patton Avenue had many Black families' homes full of children riding bikes, playing jacks in driveways, skateboarding, and playing double-dutch rope, we didn't have sidewalks to play safely like in Old Cloverdale. So it was nothing for us little Black and Brown children to take over a side street just off West Patton Avenue to throw the football, ride bikes, or compete in foot races. It was the corner of West Patton Avenue and Prairie Vista Street where we hung out and played every game we could think of playing for my crew and me. For a time, I was the only girl in a band of boys. That would eventually change when my cousins from Texas arrived for two years, which evened things a bit--3 boys and three girls. Three Hundred and Thirty-Two West Patton Avenue had a sizable crew of well-mannered and innocent little kids looking to hang out and ride our bikes.

332 W. Patton Avenue was my first home, my first love, life, and family experience. A home filled with bright smiles beaming from room to room, laughter billowing out of the windows, and hugs from arms long and strong enough to hold you to where your heartbeats synced up before you released each other. This place was where I rested my head after leaving the hospital that bright day in August. My grandparents welcomed me into the world as another Sledge extending their legacy into the future. This home on a corner lot with white siding and black shutters was the clam for our family, even up to my 2nd generation cousins and long-time family friends. From my earliest memories, anyone could always find at least 5 or 6 kids playing up and down the street on any given day. Hanging out with the crew from the block right after breakfast was the earliest my cousins and I could meet up for our daily shenanigans. Me in my scalloped shorts with the broad white trim, a cotton terry tank top, and jellies, while brandishing two ponytails and bangs, quickly riding my bike down Prairie Vista or trotting to the neighbors to see if my friends were able to play outside would be the makings of a great day.

Some days, my brother and I hung out with the Grands along with my aunt and uncle. But then there would be other cousins coming for the weekend, and it was a giant slumber party. We were always looking to have some fun when we were all there. If it wasn't riding bikes to the candy lady or sending my cousin with an order for everyone, then it was running after the ice cream truck and sometimes running to greet the arrival of a distant relative, Aunt Pauline! West Patton Avenue has more happy memories than it did/does have the opposite. As the night rolled around, girls were in my aunt's room and the boys in my uncle's room. Although there may have been almost ten people in Grandma's home at one time, their home never felt too small or that it wasn't enough space for everyone. My grandparents lived on a corner lot in a big enough home with white siding, red then changed to black shutters, a porch lined with chairs in front of the house, and a huge front and back yard. Grandma's yard was one of my favorite yards because of the high perches available to little nimble-legged people without any specific cares in the world. Heading to the Grands on the weekends with a brown paper bag of nightclothes, clean underwear, and maybe a favorite activity book was always a big event. Once we arrived at her house, I would put our bag into my aunt's room. Her room was like a young girl's room with the twin-size bed and the dresser and nightstand to match. She always had a nice comforter and pretty crochet dolls lying on her pillows.

Growing up on West Patton Avenue was the central note as I wrote my melody throughout life. Our rhythmic way of life and love was the food for my soul, and the life of that home was a perfect incubator for maturing a life force. Yet, as a child, I never imagined that the whirlwind of life would create a tug-a-war with the most authentic part of me.

Foundation

One of the first books read to me was about a little girl who captured a caterpillar on the school's playground.

At the end of the school day, she raced home, where she and her mother would place it in a jar with a twig and a leaf. The mom told her daughter that the caterpillar would soon have a magnificent change. Anxiously, the little girl waited day after day for the caterpillar to undergo this change. Her curious mind thought of all types of beautiful changes this caterpillar could make while in that jar. What could, what would become of the caterpillar? As the days went by, she noticed the caterpillar suspended in this grey web where she could barely recognize the creature. A few days later, the caterpillar was gone, and a beautiful monarch butterfly was fluttering around in the jar. She screamed, prompting her mom to witness this preternatural event. As I remember the story, the little girl didn't imagine a beautiful brightly colored butterfly would replace the caterpillar for one moment. Her mom finally arrived with a smile of satisfaction to see the caterpillar's transformation into a beautiful butterfly. She calmly explained the metamorphosis that the caterpillar underwent was due to the cycle of life and that because of this change, it was time for the little girl to release the butterfly to be free and fly.

I can still remember the crisp mornings, sleepily arriving at my grandmother's home for the day where I would climb into her chair with her and request that she read this story to me. My grandmother was my babysitter while my parents were at work. These days at grandma's house were some of the best days where I basked in the life and love of all that a proud Black family could offer a bright young inquisitive girl such as myself. After the second time we read the story together, I can remember my grandmother and me discovering some fat, green, and creepy-looking worms right outside the side of the house. She was sure to mention to me that they would become butterflies just like in the book. My big eyes looked back at her quietly, wondering if we were going to take this hair-raising creature into her house? And without skipping a beat in our lovely morning, her eyes stared back to convey...don't even ask.

I have questioned myself on this book's conscientiously sentimental value and why I was always ecstatic when my grandmother would read the book to me. Was this story moving because I could see and feel the little girl's glee after learning the caterpillar's need to transform to another stage of life? She wanted to watch the transformation, have her eyes behold the beauty of energy going through its normal process of change, mentally discriminate between when the creature was a hairy-like work and the winged beauty that will escape the protection of the clam. The difference was inevitable as long as the little girl didn't interfere with the process, and as mommy put it, the caterpillar's feat was a necessary journey of life.

As life continued, my loving grandmother Mary made her transformations on her journey. Still, I only could cherish the happiness of spending time with her doing my favorite activities, sitting with her, and sharing a book, a memory, something that we enjoyed together. I sure miss those days, but again life's journey is inevitable. Still, I'm thankful that I grew to understand beholding the beauty of transformations, just like that little girl did with the caterpillar and the butterfly, is the sheer joy that makes the journey worth it. Of course, my voyage has had several transitions, transformations, metamorphosis, and a single regeneration, all of which changed me for the better. However, the upbeat love, laughter, and life at grandma's house taught me that consistency of change keeps you strong. Strong enough to stay calm and carry on.

Before my skin had a long kiss with the Alabama sun, I had juicy thighs, pinchable cheeks both top and bottom (lol), and fair skin much like Winnie the Pooh, as I was affectionately known as Pooh, at least, that is the reason my mother provided me. Lol. I can remember that thick-thighed little girl running from the front yard to the back yard, jumping from one of my perches in the front yard to catch the next breeze around the backyard swing. We had an outdoor playset at my grandparents' home planted in the center of their enormous yard for playing, running, and climbing trees. Like clockwork, that same little girl was skipping and hopping through her world as the morning went along. I constantly climbed a tree to see above everyone else, see what others weren't looking for, and primarily just to feel the wind in my bangs. I loved being outside in my grandmother's yard. But there would be days when sitting at grandma's feet was more fun than climbing trees and wildly swinging until my body was parallel with the playset frame. Boy were those the good ole days, carefree living and a plan consisting of playing outside.

One thing about Grandma's is there was always something new and exciting happening there. Whether it was cutting grass, washing and waxing cars, a game of 21 in the driveway, or somebody just pulling up to say "Tell May Sledge, Hello," it was always something going on. I also had a young aunt, uncle, and several cousins (dually serving as babysitters) that I have always felt were my older brothers and sisters because we were raised together on West Patton Avenue.

Grandma's house was always the spot. She and my Grandfather had a large corner lot with enough yard to run and play for every hour of a long southern summer day. Even on the days that I stayed inside with her, I still had fun. It was probably the best fun I'd have because it was a sacred moment we shared where I understood what made her, her. She'd share stories of her childhood, reminisce on her life as a young girl, a young woman, and a mother. I remember times when we'd gone through her jewelry box, where she gave a story for each piece. I listened to each memory of my Granddad showering her with gifts, always adorning her with trinkets showing how much she meant to him. Mary treasured those memories with my grandfather. Finally, Grandma chuckled one day and said that she'd look at her jewelry box to remind her of her love of him, her life with him, and his love for her and their life together.

This grand woman, my grandmother, was my idol. I looked at her in awe. How beautifully, sassy, sweet, dainty, and strong was she? I watched her efficiently run her home and simultaneously serve as a fiercely loyal helpmate to her husband. Home management was an integral position not taken lightly. Mainly because home management was the foundation of your family and specifically the rearing of children, Black moms and grandmothers invested all they could muster into protecting their tribes. West Patton Ave, the home of a proper Southern Girl's tutelage (leading a god-fearing life alongside the spirit of advocacy), carried rooms filled with memories of life lessons, laughter, and Grandma singing her favorite hymns...I surrender all. It all reminds me that these aspects are the trappings of a humble and loving family. Grandma's form of love ensnared everyone that came through the front door.

One year, my father and uncles refurbished the back porch as a den for Ms. Mary. This additional room was in response to my grandfather having developed emphysema and the requirement of continuous use of a portable oxygen tank. So, of course, the den was complete with a navy blue couch, a tan-striped chair for me, books, all of her favorite things, and the television. The den was a time machine, a portal into a different world. Though we would often discuss a news article, oblige questions on the day's status, television to watch our favorite shows: Wheel of Fortune, The Rockford Files, Jeopardy, and Golden Girls (her favorite was Blanche...), we always felt that this was our room. *Our den* to discuss *our thoughts* on the past, present, and future; an opportunity to escape into treasured memories. It was those long hot Alabama Summer days that rolled into peaceful, refreshing Fall evenings when we shared our stories and discussed the days' breaking news while eating homemade cracklin'.

As the summers continued to pass us by with frolicked laughter in the wind and a hug from the warmth of the evening sky, I would find myself pondering on inquiries for the next day after breakfast and my morning chores. It was apparent the previous day's questions would spawn my queries. But this meant no time for flag football or racing bikes with my brother and cousins and minimal time climbing trees. Honestly, I was outgrowing my tomboy proclivities as she would whisper with a snarky side glance as I'd squeak by her over the threshold of the front door.

Cool afternoons when we couldn't spend those quaint times together and my BFF next door wasn't home, Ms. Mary would find me asleep on her front porch. Sleeping on the front porch was the most refreshing nap. I have not had naps like those since we sold that house. Usually, there was no problem with this porch activity, but my youngest aunt bought me a denim mini-skirt this particular summer. Because it was from my aunt, I fell in love with the skirt. Now, I'd never focused on my figure or saw anything but Pooh when I looked at my reflection. *My primary function for the full-length mirror in the hallway was for lip-syncing to The Wiz, Xanadu, or my little dialogue (when I was in need to work out some situation in my head first).* So, after the mini-skirt fitting session, I found myself looking in the mirror at a reflection in a different view than before.

And Mary perceived it was time for me to acknowledge my magic or, in her words, my beautiful self and not be distracted by things less important in life.

Once on a relaxed afternoon, Ms. Mary noticed that I had fallen asleep on the porch, so she beckoned me inside, real matter-of-fact-like. I could tell from her even tone that she was not asking or making a request, but it was vital for me to come inside. So, sleepily, I walked to the back room affectionately known to us as our meeting place, a sort of watering hole of sorts if you will, to plop down in my chair next to her only to notice a small box that was new to me but I could see it was very familiar to her. My visage immediately lightened with a wrinkle in my smile and sparkle in my eyes. Because I knew this would be a talk between her and me about a new and intriguing world to me but familiar, unfinished, and a place she desired to share with me.

Ms. Mary pulled out a tattered black and white picture of a dark-skinned woman with shoulder-length hair and piercing eyes dressed in a light-colored dress that was cinched at the waist. When I inquired about this woman, my grandmother's supposition tickled my ears when she announced this woman she believed to be her mother. Her slender vascular fingers swiped the front of the picture as my eyes followed the lines of her high cheekbones, round face, almond-shaped eyes, and proud lips. So this woman was her mother?

And before I could inquire as to her grandness, Ms. Mary informed me that she was hard-working and always came to get her at the end of the day to go home and get dinner. Her mother picked cotton while she played outside. She didn't know precisely what or where her mother would be picking cotton but always knew she'd return from the fields to get her at the end of the day. As she viewed the picture, she remembered her mother's stern words about the kids in her class making fun of her appearance and causing her to cry and dread a return to school ever again. Her mother sharply explained that she should never be ashamed of who she is or her looks. Her words...*don't be afraid of who you are because you are perfect in your beauty, and if you are, then you are afraid and ashamed of me because you came from me. Walk with your head held high and shoulders back like the lady you are because you come from good stock.*

Reminiscing about her school days brought Ms. Mary to ask about my own, especially my newfound love for the violin. She delighted in my quest to be a violinist. My teacher at the time had already proclaimed that I was already a promising violinist. I would always inform her of my Tour de Force in the orchestra and the symphony nights. My first visit to the symphony orchestra was at the Alabama Theatre, and Ms. Mary had a story about now being able to go inside and watch shows from across the street. She was excited to hear about her granddaughter's trailblazing in life where she was never able to. After every violin story, I'd invite her to my shows or request extra tickets for her and granddaddy to attend. He had to travel with oxygen, so they weren't able to participate with us most of the time. This one late October afternoon, I had a performance in the old Cloverdale community, and Ms. Mary would be in attendance. It was vital for her to see me frolicking about in my world because she'd shared so much of her world with me; I longed for us to share this present world. I will never forget that performance. I was the first chair in the 2nd violin section (moving my way up to the first chair). I could see her soft and proud smile beaming on stage. Amazingly my fingers were the most agile they'd ever been tapping over the fingerboard delightfully as every cell in my body was gleeful as she watched from the right behind the orchestra pit. I couldn't believe how empowered I felt from her visit to my world outside W. Patton Avenue. After the show, I was the proud recipient of the most prestigious award of the night, a breath-taking hug from my grandmother as she shouted how proud she was of me that night. I have lived for that night repeatedly over the years. Every time I accomplish a goal, I think about my grandmother's smile and the bear hug she'd give me. She hadn't realized that night, and neither did I, for that matter, at least not in the terms that I do now because empowerment is the best gift to give to a young black girl realizing her dreams in the world. I hope she knows that she became the wind beneath my wings at that very moment in life.

Soon our time was cut short. My time with Ms. Mary was not as long as I would have liked due to her health. Ms. Mary was a smoker and suffered from an aneurysm. But because of the memories of time spent in that home, I hadn't even realized how it helped me to learn how to roll with the punches, be resilient, walk tall even when you should be afraid or cringe, and most importantly, don't give up if it's within your power to make something happen.

As life continued, nearly thirty years later is when an inquisitive soul helped me acknowledge that Ms. Mary has been smiling every time I've been blessed to discover a pearl from the hardships of my journey. And the mere thought of her watchful eye and soft voice humming in my memory takes me home every single time.

Soon as I get home

In a different place

In a different time

Different people around me

I would like to know of that different world

And how different they find me...

Soon as I get home

Part II

Resilience

Fortitude*Family*Friends

All my work, my life, everything I do is about
survival, not just bare, awful, plodding
survival, but survival with grace and faith.
While one may encounter many defeats, one
must not be defeated.
Maya Angelou

*"Come, listen to a story about a lady named Dori, a recent graduate tryin'
to make it in this world. In the search for some work, she cast a wide net,
and to her surprise came a note from FCPS. Virginia that is, Autism
Program, Co-Pilot Teacher. Well, the next thing you know, Dori's moving
on up. Her kinfolk said, don't move away from here. They said Alabama
is the place you ought to be, but she loaded up the car and moved to the
DMV. Alexandria, that is. Politicos and the Beltway." [Beverly Hillbillies
tune].*

It's December; master's in hand, and eager to teach, but no open
positions for special education teachers with Applied Behavior
Analysis/Autism background. My significant other at the time advised me
to apply to schools everywhere that looked interesting and where some
family was in the vicinity. Fairfax County Public Schools of Northern
Virginia gave me a call within a week. Upon notice of the position, I had
two non-negotiables: interview by Jan. 8th and report to work by Jan. 25[th.]
With a determined mindset to bet on me, I knew it was my responsibility
to my family to accept the job offer and move to Virginia.

It was a good fortune with a salary three times what 1st-year teachers
make in Alabama or Georgia. But, with only one income and two weeks
to prepare, what were we going to do about housing before we got
there? Everything was a lengthy process, including our pay. My Alabama
clan and I catapulted ourselves right into some scary territory of limited
access to housing in an unfamiliar land. Sowing seeds of foundation

anywhere outside of Alabama was an adventure for each of us. Upon arriving in Virginia, we had no home to rest our heads or a place for restoration after Alexandria, Virginia's long cold winter days. Tyree and I were plump with hope while embracing our adventure with unbridled courage as we set out for the DC, Maryland, and Virginia metropolitan areas.

As graduation or parting gift from Auburn University, each graduate had complimentary hotel stays and car rentals. This gesture was our initial saving grace, the temporary reservations at a cheap hotel along route 1 in Alexandria and only a couple grand in our pockets. We weren't sure how far it would take us, but we had a dream, and failure, i.e., homelessness, was not going to get in the way. At least that's how we approached it until homelessness was staring us squarely in the face. Then, as a woman with a strong faith passed down from Mary Sledge, I knew that my mindset was vital to achieving any goal.

Typically, being a planner, this adventure would have been planned much differently with a preselected home in a pleasant environment for Karma to play and make friends. But as God would have it, I needed to have faith the size of a mustard seed and move as instructed. My spirit assured me that it would all unfold as we embarked on this journey if I continued to believe in the dream.

So we set off on Interstate 85 North through Atlanta, Georgia and Greenville, South Carolina towards Petersburg, Virginia, then onto

Alexandria, Virginia. Based on the GPS to Fort Belvoir, VA, the January 8th interview from Auburn to Alexandria would take us about 13 hours to complete. We had a five-year-old in tow, and we would need breaks to use the restroom and stretch her juicy little legs. At least that is what we planned as responsible and considerate parents, but would you believe that Karma slept most of the time. I remember her waking just as we came to Spotsylvania. "Mommy! Look at the snow. It's snowing.", said Karma with an unusually high-pitched five-year-old voice. As I responded with an affirmative, my anxiety began to rise because we were in no way prepared for snow on our first night here. See, back in central Alabama (Montgomery, Tuskegee, Auburn, and Sylacauga areas), we don't get snow in amounts where citizens are expected to drive in it. And as southern, as I'd like to consider myself, I knew that neither Tyree nor myself were familiar with moving in snow-like or snowy conditions. But Karma was ecstatic about the whole notion of snow and the possibility of seeing and playing for that matter in it regularly. Seeing her get excited about the snow helped to ease my thoughts.

Leaving Alabama was hard for Karma because, as an only child, she didn't have any siblings to bond with, and most of her cousins lived a nice little distance away from us and our parents' homes. She was too young to remember her little friends in Sylacauga and had just acquired a best friend that lived in our neighborhood. They rode the bus together every day and even had the same Kindergarten teacher at Auburn Early Education Center, Ms. Cutler. I can remember our daily routines starting at the bus stop. Precious and her mom approached us as we waited just like any regular school morning. As the girls shared greetings and began to retell their five-year-old adventures from the evening before, she and I spoke about our move to Virginia. Both girls in the earshot of the discussion started to hug each other and consider the possibility of the breakup of the friendship. As caring mothers, we assured the girls that they didn't have to end the friendship and that we live in a new age of cell phones and the internet. Looking back now, who were we to tell these millennials about the internet and cell phones? So later that week, as we traveled the road to Virginia in our little white Hyundai, I reflected on the sacrifices of my family to support my dream. It was my dream for the family I created, just the three of us.

Karma sacrificed her newfound relationships for this dream; a five-year-old who is just learning how to be social with others must now start at the beginning of things again with a whole new group of people that are the least bit aware of the type of life and family she had left to begin anew over 900 miles away. She is already a shy girl with curly locs on her shoulders; she has always been academically advanced for her age. Soon, her teachers would discover her high achievement came with a mild case of ADHD, which I creatively managed via her diet. Her arrival in VA was as the baby on Sacajawea's backpack as she led Lewis and Clark across the Mississippi and the Rocky Mountains going west. She was in tow of these two parents of hers and was just following where they led. She didn't complain much outside of the tears for her friend, Precious. Karma was a trooper, and she didn't whine while on the ride, and when we got to her new school, she didn't shy away from the teacher or the class, and she continued to make good grades in school. And unlike some children, the transition didn't significantly impact her at home or school. Being a first-time mom, this journey with Karma proved to me that children are very resilient. She wasn't afraid to take this leap of faith with her parents and did it with vibrant expectations.

Tyree was much different from Karma in that he was ready to leave the South and venture into a world of opportunity that the DMV could possibly offer. Albeit, his sacrifice would be similar to Karma's sacrifice, family, and friendships. He enjoyed his fair share of friends and family, but this move would put him out of reach and on a hustle that didn't permit any time for catching up with buddies. This move required him to hustle for better employment, be the primary caregiver for Karma while I was in the classroom all day, hustle to secure our housing, and all before pick up from school. But most importantly, he and I had to be reconciled to one another as husband and wife. The holidays, the first half of the winter that year in Auburn, held mountains and valleys similar to those on the rollercoaster ride, the Scream Machine at Six Flags. Our relationship had endured many hurdles before our adventure to the DMV; however, our last fight almost cost me my 3.5 GPA in grad school and preparation for the defense of my comps and final exams. So for me, I was ready to leave, but with him, not so much.

Two months before our January trek to the DMV, I was preparing for mass educator interviews with local school districts looking to complete their teaching staff for the school year. I went to the Ashley Stuart in the mall in my neighborhood and purchased a very nice blue suit with a woven jacket and navy blue pleated ruffled skirt. With my portfolio in hand and confidence on the brain, as I step to the convention center doors, I catch a glimpse of Tyree walking in my direction, clothed in some dusty jeans and tee shirt with a backpack. Once he spots me, he motions for me to speak with him, and I notice he looks very messy and confused. "Hey Dori, what are you doing here?" he said sheepishly. "Well, if you must know, I am preparing for interviews so that I can find a position," I exclaimed. "Here?" He asks. "Anywhere that is singing the right salary and located within a nice district." I retorted. "So, are you taking my baby with you?" "Of course, I am taking my baby with me." "Well, you just can't take my baby away from me. "I can if you are not taking care of her."

This brief discussion between us that day changed his life. Since Karma's conception, Tyree had been overjoyed by the mere thought of Karma's birth and to realize, at that moment, that she could possibly live and grow in another city without his consistent presence in her life. But he and we struggled to get a sure footing in the marriage and parenting game. His battle with addiction while juggling the responsibilities and expectations of being married and being a new father was a hurdle that was difficult to jump over. Neither of us hadn't had any schooling sufficient to guide us towards a more resilient foundation or with the tools to handle the illness destroying our marriage. But after he saw the grit in my countenance as a result of his actions towards our family unit, Tyree got himself together with sustainable employment and secured our home in Alexandria. Seemingly, he was determined to commit to our family again. A total mind shift of growth both together and individually fueled the launch of this journey.

After we made it to Alexandria, every *Plan A* we created had fallen through, and it was back to strategizing how we were going to make it in this big city. Rainy and cold with ice piled up as little white caps of a mountain range on the side of the road or as maze markers throughout the parking lots was a familiar setting for the next two weeks. In Alabama, we'd never experienced anything such as this type of weather. I looked over at the mounds of snow and ice while sitting in the car discussing our next moves and immediately questioned all of that grit I had back in Auburn. The week hadn't been the best, and I began to doubt the choice I made.

Never in my wildest dreams would I imagine my previous work in social services would arm me with a savviness for connecting resources for at-risk situations. Before arriving in Virginia, I signed up for the New Teacher's Home program; we learned that the funds had been exhausted upon our arrival. Thank God for Google because it led me to and Good Shepherd Housing had a waiting list. I remembered upon graduation Auburn gifted 3 Free night stays at Choice motels, but you had to sleep three nights first. Our money ran out quickly those first two weeks. Thank God for smartphones because I found a pantry to get some fruit and bread and a few perishables, i.e., PB&J and juice. By the end of the first month, Tyree worked and proved himself worthy of promotion as a store manager of Office Depot. We had "down-home" connections with his manager. She, too, from Alabama, became a part of our village and connected us with additional resources such as transportation and some good ole home cooking now and again. This hustle to get settled comfortably for ourselves and this new way of life helped us keep our minds on our grind. They say the best way to eat an elephant-sized problem is with one bite at a time. We were building bones of resilience with this journey filled with lifelong lessons.

Hebrews 11:1 Now faith is the substance of things hoped for and the evidence of things unseen.

Black Southern Belles have a deep connection with spirituality and faith in God. As a woman of the south, a relationship with God and the belief that you have the power to move mountains is a prerequisite for success and longevity. I have been witness to many miracles both personally and within my community. Praying to God, meditating on His Word, and believing that the impossible can and will happen is the work you must put into the dream. Northern Virginia, Alexandria, more specifically, was our new little place on the earth. But it was difficult to smooth things out in the dead of winter and with just the 3 in our little family. People didn't seem as friendly as back home in Alabama; I would see people out in the community, I'd smile or speak, and nothing would part their lips. I would encounter African American women that would frown if I spoke to them. I couldn't help but think that area of the country couldn't be the right place for me because everyone is disgruntled, and I don't want to spend the next few years learning to accept this kind of engagement as standard.

Yes, we can

Yours and mine [?]

Yes, we can

Are one and one equals three

Yes, we can

I feel it like lightning in the forest

Yes, we can

And they can know, they can see the woman as a chorus

You're my woman, don't need another

Get behind the other; we can lift each other

Tornado weather, we another level

Don't you know that we're able to?

Let alone makes us major.

We can now sit at the table

And grow in his favor

"I am tired! I want to go back home. I don't like it here, and it's ok if we go back home, right?" I said to Tyree as we sat in that white Hyundai among those white mountain ranges in the parking lot. Before I could get the last part out, he turned my face towards his and looked squarely in the eye, and said, "No! We are not going back home. WE WILL DO JUST

FINE right here in Alexandria. So if you need to finish this cry, go right ahead, right here. But after this, NO MORE CRYING." Tyree's voice was low, stern, and matter-of-fact. This Tyree was the guy I remembered from Birmingham, Alabama.

I hadn't seen him in a long while, and even amid my bawling of despair, it was encouraging to hear this confidence come from him. But things didn't look up overnight. Next, our transportation hit the bricks. By the time the snow started to melt, and the trees began to have tiny green buds all over, it seemed that we encountered another situation requiring strategic planning. I worked about 2 miles from home but on the military installation. So, I couldn't just walk on base to teach; Karma and I would need to access the school campus. Now, back home, this would not have been a likely scenario that would have required a creative resolution; however, any notion of returning home was NOT an option. So I would need to figure it out. Then, I needed to suit up to play ball, and there's no crying baseball.

When this issue arose, I just knew this was a sign that we needed to go home. So Friday afternoon, Karma and I arrive home from school, tired and hungry. Tyree, still in his Office Depot uniform while standing in the fridge as though he was having a male summer, saw my long face. "All I need you to do is keep teaching and make sure that fat baby is alright. We are NOT, absolutely not going back home. We are tough enough to make it just as we planned." Trying to teach a class full of students close to your daughter's age and trying to juggle the many hats that mothers usually do was a feat in and of itself. Nothing new to most mothers, just new to novice mothers. And I was her, that new mother in a new land intending to make things familiar but still in the phase of exploration and deciphering what feels right and what suits me. But faith that God didn't place this seed as a dream deferred, I figured out a plan of attack because that was my only option. So a week before payday, we signed the papers at home and went to sleep on pillows of peace. Our days had to begin early, 5:30 am for me and 6 am for Karma. My school was an extended day school. Being a new teacher on campus and a part of a pilot program, my vision was to put my best into running this enhanced Autism program to show that FCPS didn't make a mistake when bringing me onboard in late January.

It was Daylight Savings in early March; the night sky continued to linger by the time we'd walk to the bus stop to catch the Richmond Highway Dart. Karma, five years old with short thick thighs and a creative and inquisitive mind, set out with me every morning for the next two weeks on the Dart, then about ½ a mile further to the doors of the school. A little short on stature but big on imagination, Karma was a trooper during this time. Her brown eyes were big with excitement and a smile that wouldn't quit. I thought that she would be disappointed in the change in our routine given our circumstances, but this time is one of my best stories about my baby girl and me. For Karma, catching the bus was an adventure. So she'd see new people that she was always ready to offer a smile and a soft hello. As afraid as I was about her friendliness, I remembered how she was being raised to speak to people and offer a friendly hello. It never hurts to speak to someone. My grandmother's pearl of wisdom, "Be not forgetful to entertain strangers: for thereby some have entertained angels unawares." Hebrews 13:2 KJV. I am sure that Karma wasn't thinking this entirely when she spoke, but I would remind her to keep it brief with a slight squeeze and the intent to hold her hand in mine. There were seven stops until the final one that put us the closest to the school as we approached the gate.

This week was St. Patrick's week, and the Kinders at school had a leprechaun activity where Karma and I had to build a trap. Enamored with the notion of a leprechaun, I created an adventure in our walks to school from the last stop, just as I would have figured that her little legs may be tired of the travel. We began to cross a field where the grass was patchy but not too muddy given the winter. "Hey Karma, did you see that leprechaun just now over that small ridge?" As I pointed off in the distance. Immediately her big eyes were searching desperately for the character to appear. We kept walking, and I noticed her curious demeanor. "If he sees us, he will get us. He will capture us, and Daddy won't be able to find us. " Kama replied to my prior inquiry. I know, so if we see him again, we have to run. Can you do that so that we can make it to school?" She nodded without even looking at me. Karma was still looking for the leprechaun and unwilling to allow him to catch us and keep us. LOL.

This bump in the road didn't stop our little family that could; this experience displayed our Sparkle in the entire ordeal. It was a sign that we'd count it all joy pretty soon. After two weeks of outsmarting the leprechauns, we went to purchase a classic Volvo 240D that was perfect for our troop with space for luggage and an engine for travel. The pieces were coming together as long as we believed.

If we believed in ourselves and each other, we'd thrive. Our adventure required not only faith but reciprocity of love, encouragement, and reinforcement of tradition, specifically between Tyree and myself. What did we have within us to grow? How did our environment/village support our successes and failures? Did we acknowledge our wins to uplift our dispositions that would equip us to continue building a legacy?

The lesson we learned about Resiliency is that many factors influence its growth. Factors such as positive support, the environment, and recurring positive events build self-efficacy, thus maintaining resilient behavior. After over ten years in the DMV, many wins from lessons learned have helped build self-efficacy levels over the years.

Tend to your own Garden?

"And everything that I have planted has grown. And all it needed was time, earth, water, and the sunlight" -- Corrine Bailey Rae, Green Aphrodisiac.

This statement captures the essence of intimate comrades such as the family, friends, and old flames, three categories of people that will always have a purpose, a lesson, or a much-needed blessing in your life. Throughout my lifetime, I have realized that the ones in your life for a season are those past loves that inspire you to know what good love feels like to you.

Being a girl from the South, my family and I are no strangers to nature or animals. And when you are familiar with living things outside of humans, you grow to understand the reciprocity and the rhythm of life. For instance, a vegetable farmer knows that if he doesn't till his ground, his seeds aren't likely to germinate; his crop will likely get blown away in the wind or eaten by vermin, and his harvest will be non-existent. Most vegetable farmers also learn of a technique called rhythm farming. This is a technique where farmers follow the cycle or rhythm of the soil to get the best crop that will feed his family. Being a Black and Southern girl (which differs from a traditional Southern Belle), I know that the rhythm of the soil is essential to understand, get familiar with it and be responsive to it. The whole seed, plant, harvest, repeat is a complimentary rally between man and Mother Earth. They must dance gracefully to be successful. I lived in Sylacauga, Alabama, a rural town about 20 minutes from Auburn, 45 minutes from Birmingham, an hour from Montgomery, and about 90 minutes from Atlanta. It's a quaint little town where downtown shops close early because of the Wednesday night Bible Study on Wednesdays. What I enjoyed the most about living there was the city's greenery. There was greenery for as far as your eye could see almost in any direction of the town. Sylacauga is best known for its natural marble quarry, but you will also find many small-sized farmers. Farmers who are pretty familiar with farming rhythms and understand this rhythm impact so many different aspects of their lives, such as what we eat and when we can eat it.

When I reminisce of this specific dance, my love for the farmer's market, and the men a part of my foundation, I am often reminded of the word husband, another name for a woman's male spouse. Another definition of the word is to manage and conserve resources. Both purposes can be relative to the management of a relationship. As a side note, husband, meaning farmer was around long before the word husband used in the combination of man and wife. So in our society, we can presuppose that husband is a derivative definition to husbandry/farmer. And this derivation can be seen in two relationships that I observed throughout my journey. Both my father and grandfather were my representations of good men and good husbands. Not that they were without faults because we all are imperfect, but they were invested. Each man made a covenant with God and his legacy to be in the game until the end. And their relationships with their wives were a dance. Their countenance demonstrated confidence I haven't found in guys today. The dance resembles the farming rhythm where you till the ground, plant the seed, harvest, and repeat. My father showed me that a man should pour into his woman, the lady he loves, manifest her true self, and enhance his harvest. My father believed that a man should see his woman like a flower. Not only is the woman his treasure, but her beauty exudes through her intelligence, ingenuity, and intrigue. To have a woman as a partner such as my mother was a winning event. My mother is ingenious, intelligent, and intriguing, and he knew that then and knows that now, hence their long and enduring marriage. A small-statured woman with African features like her father walked with a switch because of the pronounced curvature in her legs. My mom's great legs usually took a heel to accentuate, especially in a pencil skirt. As I reflect on my parent's marriage, I remember my father would get in a musical mood and play all of his favorite love songs from Stevie Wonder, EWF, The Temptations, Marvin Gaye, Prince, and even Rose Royce.

The Ridgecrest community, especially along W. Patton Avenue, had mostly two-parent households; at least the children we played with had both sets of parents or grandparents in their home. And that meant that in our eyes, there was family, there was support, there was a clan of folks that love you.

The first handsome man I'd ever met, I can remember his bright smile and knew precisely why mom was smitten with him. *(They've always been the cutest couple to me, both just as young at heart as they've always been).* Tall, dark-skinned, kind, and sweet, I get my romantic side from him from listening to him woo my mom on Saturday afternoons with all of his balladeers from the sixties and seventies music and then meet her in the kitchen to serenade her all while whisking her around the room. They always had a rhythm of their own, from Saturday serenades to our daily routines. With limber movements and familiar feet, there were no out-of-step routines or missteps to ruin the moment, just the giggles of my mother.

A five-foot-three stature sashayed down the hallway after trying on a white A-line dress just before its finishing touches. It was my mom taking a look at her work thus far on her dress for the matrons. It was a classic pattern with an open slit neckline, long sleeves, a gathered waist, and tea-dress length. I loved those dresses on her. The Mrs. Cleaver style of clothing is a very flattering dress, I think for a lady. And my mother wore them well. A great sashay requires an excellent heel, meaning that the tea-length dress should have a heel height of at least 3 inches when considering a vibrant young woman. And Deloris didn't disappoint, not one time. If it's one thing that I get from my mom, it is my swag! She went everywhere like she owned the place, at least that's how it appeared to me. When she wore one of her dresses, With a confident strut in any dress she wore, my Dad definitely was always the proudest man to have the best Belle with him. Their rhythms complimented each other.

"We have each other In so many ways

We'll have each other from now on

I keep feelin you I keep feelin you

Every single day baby I keep feelin you"

Songwriters: Frankie Beverly Feel That You're Feelin' lyrics © Kobalt Music Publishing Ltd.

But only a man that can connect with his woman's rhythm can embrace her power. He must be familiar with her inner thoughts and informed on her life source separate from him. What is his woman outside of him? Many men mentally skip this part and miss out on a passionate relationship with the love of his life. Asking himself what he can't live without at this time? Most men get distracted from completing this objective as he partakes on the journey with his woman. Achieving this objective doesn't happen overnight; it doesn't take 5 to 6 or 10 years either but provides a relationship with a unique dance to their rhythm. A melody that he owns the royalties to if he plays his hand right. And because this insight into his woman's essence requires this awareness, he can feel the rhythm of this dance.

In May, my parents came to visit and decided to go downtown for some shopping. It was a warm day, and I wore one of my favorite summer dresses, light blue with soft yellow flowers and some patent leather thong sandals; mom and my daughter were in jeans and tee-shirts, and my dad was in a tee and shorts. That's his regular mode, relaxed and calm. His perspective on my mother was to *take care of her so that she can take care of him*. It was at that moment, as we crossed that hot and crowded G Street, NW, to visit the watch vendor, that I realized that he'd always had this perspective when it comes to my mother. His inflection in that statement was as though the message was knowledge of only wise men. These husbands had endured times when the melody was choppy, staccato-like, or even when there had been areas of rest where all the music stopped, but thankfully it was brief. His warning was as though only men worthy of their bond knew this to be so. I smiled as I listened to his speech; my pupils dilated just as a baby sees a lovely face because those words reaffirmed that he still feels her rhythm. His speech reminded me of what he taught me so many years ago about love. I missed the days when I could listen to my dad's perspective on life.

If you know anything about True Black Southern Belles, we are 99.999% Daddy's Girl no matter what, meaning that we have learned of our worth early in life. Given this perspective, I treasure his insight. I grew to observe him always finding a way to stay committed to the rhythm between them by pouring into her.

This warm summer-like day in May, brought to mind all of the times I watched my mom gleefully smile because my father engineered a surprise. First, coolly, he'd revealed how he'd' been listening to her symphony, the percussion, her strings, and brass sections. Then, he'd fine-tuned the syncopation of the rhythm to fit their steps more succinctly. The memories of these moments always had mom giddy and smiling from ear to ear like a high school crush. These memories were the seeds germinating my dreams of being with the love of my life forever.

This "feeling her rhythm" brings memories to my mind of another man, my grandfather. He and my grandmother were perfect dance partners. Ms. Mary was a tiny thing compared to Mr. Sledge; she fit right under his arm and close to his side. My grandfather always appeared to be a giant over us all. He was always taller than everyone; he wore slacks, a collared shirt with suspenders capped with wingtips, or black loafers. On Saturdays, while hanging out on West Patton Ave, Mr. Sledge usually dozed off in his lounge chair. His favorite show played in the background, usually baseball or Matlock on the floor model TV. This particular Saturday afternoon, hanging out with my granddad in the family room, then came Ms. Mary. I can still hear her quick-stepping through the kitchen and just past his lounge chair announcing that she'd be going to play Pokeno with her girlfriends at 6:30 pm. To my ears, her announcement meant Paul, "I'm about to leave as I mentioned or as you should be aware." But my grandparents knew that it meant, don't forget, that I am leaving and will need some seed money for this venture. She kissed him tenderly on the forehead as she passed him and went to prepare for her outing. And sure enough, as she was ready to leave, Paul motioned for her to get his money clip so that she could be on her way. One part of their melody was that Paul was aware of Mary's days of cooking for him and two handfuls of children, cleaning and watching those grands over for the weekend. All on behalf of the family, correct? Observing an environment where grandma had the space to do what she felt was essential to maintain her sense of self was critical in my self-concept of routine self-care.   Routinely, my grandfather's dance moves within their waltz kept the music flowing. And just as my father had advised years later, if he loves his woman in the language she speaks, she will love him as he needs her to do.

The Millennial-like phrase for this type of intimacy is known as Love Reciprocity. It's the name of the tune, and it is distinct for every couple. Love Reciprocity is when people invest in their relationship. When something is important enough, we all know it will emotionally connect partners to build and maintain relationships. "Reciprocated love and emotional contributions are behavioral investments that sustain a committed relationship." Anne Ream, ATR-BC, LPC in Good Therapy (July 12, 2010). Over the years, I would attest to their great love and that of my parents and other couples in our community loving the reciprocal response of a natural rhythm of their own. But over and above many couples, these two enduring relationships added even more enrichment to my womanhood and my concept of love.

And let's consider my concept of love and how I'd apply or didn't apply what I thought I learned. My thoughts on love have evolved over the years, which is expected as one matures and incorporates life experiences and practical implications from those experiences. But by the time I had been married, my concept of love was still an immature perspective. Immature in the aspect of the notion that I didn't have a fully developed sense of the steps in the middle. I was missing the drumline of our melody, that syncopation of our love that would drive the piece through to the end or at least over, under, and through crescendos, decrescendos, and staccato rallies along the journey. Hindsight is 20/20, right? And my hindsight provided a clearer picture of the issues in our marriage.

We met in undergraduate school at UAB, Karma's dad and I did. Unbeknownst to me, the story goes that he had his eye on me for quite some time. As it happens between an Alpha woman and an Alpha man, I remembered what my grandmother taught me...allow him to pursue and make a choice.

We had more than our fair share of struggles, whether organic or self-sabotage, and I am not sure any couple could have survived even with the best counselor around to provide support. And I think we could feel the weight of it all subconsciously, hence the continued friction. He and I were keen on the result of two people coming together supposedly in love, but we were oblivious to the best approach to get there. We were just two egotistical kids begrudgingly shouting at each other, "I want this, not that!". He and I have spoken on numerous occasions about what our issues were in the marriage. Yes, we struggled with communication, just like *Malcolm and Marie*, 2020. When heated or particularly focused, our verbal communication was similar to the shouting scenes between this couple. We deeply felt that our communication was not the best approach in our relationship. Still, we struggled with correcting the course because we were afraid to be vulnerable to each other.

When communication is not adequate, doesn't land well, misses the point, or focuses on a topic that is not pertinent to communication. The communication options are limited and often negative, especially with two *stubbornnaries* (like luminaries), not stubborn Aries (though he is an Aries!). Leigh Noren, MSc, in Thrive Global's community section, discusses the importance of communication to build intimacy between people. It's the vehicle to meeting needs and establishing a relationship for couples. However, communication requires a level of vulnerability. Vulnerability is typically the culprit when a connection is on the fritz or ends altogether with animus parties. It is also not something outsiders can readily identify in a couple unless they have intimate regular engagements. Meaning, the couples would share some of their private feelings with another couple, such as best friends or church members. So, though as a youngin' I delighted in the notion of both my parents and my grandparents' rhythm, I was not privy to the vulnerability that is/was required to maintain such love songs. In the South, we have a saying, "Children need to stay [sic] in a child's place." So my limited knowledge did not provide me with any of the actual "ins and outs" of their relationship. These critical facts were unknown to me, and thus I missed vital information required to implement the same sentiments into my marriage when it was time to do so.

After several years of attempting to solve our relationship issues, one argument became a most illuminating moment in our lives. I mentioned to him that we were going about our course of action as though when we argue, it's as though we chose to deal with the caricature of the other person. We'd lost the insight to tend to one another in ways that promoted growth. Falling prey to the power couple syndrome of securing our independent professional footing was a detour off the main road. Instead of intentionally tilling the soil of our relationship, we had this crazy idea that resenting each other for negligence would get the tilling completed, and our marriage would eventually get better.

This very day, my ex-husband will note that this statement was the most illuminating perspective on our relationship that it helped him change his perspective on how he approached each time we engaged the other. This change in attitude added a layer of accountability to both partners. Still, it was too little too late for us as a married couple, given that the main issue for divorce proved to be impervious to this newfound tactic of effective communication and intimate level of vulnerability.

To be vulnerable is to be brave. Vulnerability is to yield to the other in trust and be confident in your skin to support the other. It is a complex personality trait to manage and to project when developing intimate relationships. Vulnerability is not the opposite of strength; it's a necessary part. We have to force ourselves to open up and expose ourselves and offer up everything we have. And just pray that it's good enough. Otherwise, we will never succeed in anything of substance or that matters. This is true when looking for love.

FAILURE and FORGIVENESS

Forgiveness: They say that forgiveness is for you, not the other person. People I've forgiven most recently: Myself—I remember reading a romance novel where Table for Two, where the main characters had a marriage, were top professionals in their careers, nice digs, and no children. Did I mention that they were aesthetically beautiful and aware of their intrinsic draw to others? The female lead was a globetrotter, vibrant and sharp as can be in her field. As a young girl, that was my dream. I could see myself living this life as an adult. I went through grade school and Undergraduate school; I fantasized about my life mirroring Summer Lyndon's jet-setting life with a beautiful love, husband, and career. My thoughts were to set up this notion to be successful, have a great love, and see the world.

One thing that is great about being a Black Woman from the South is, she maintains a strength that grows in concrete. It's not a strength that you initially recognize because it appears that this strength is normal, naturally expected, and very commonplace. But initially, a young child doesn't understand the need to exercise this internal strength to build and maintain muscle regularly. Still, when it comes naturally, you're not aware of the need to continue the exercise and the work you need to put in. Janet Jackson said, "I'm convinced that we Black women possess a special indestructible strength that allows us to not only get down, but to get up, to get through, and to get over." But by the time I had a 15-year relationship with marriage, family, and friends, the looming shadow of my marriage's failure was a formidable giant.

Nina Simone: WHAT KEPT ME SANE WAS KNOWING THINGS WOULD CHANGE, AND IT WAS A QUESTION OF KEEPING MYSELF TOGETHER UNTIL THEY DID.

What is forgiveness? When I finally understood that forgiveness in my life is and will always be about *ME*, my events and environment took a different color. Let me give you some context about my tussle with forgiveness. This next journey of my life was almost the cote de gras for my Table for Two dreams. Notwithstanding, my heartbeat decided to take on a more physical representation of life and love. Before those ten years of life, love, and travel, my marriage was facing a demise of its own. As any woman can tell you, divorce is not for the faint at heart, even with lovers' turned spouses or best-friends turned spouses. Divorce-this time was the bleakest time of my life in that I was not a person that failed at my endeavors. Success on my goals didn't come too tricky for me, and boy, I felt that I had put in quite some time and effort with this one. At the beginning of this arduous excursion, I can remember the days crying myself to sleep, tears on the horizon, and tears in my wine. My sad rounds of phone therapy with my best friend on how this could be happening to me and why would it be this were also exhausting? The death of a thing.

Brene´ Brown states in "Rising Strong" that forgiveness is the death of something. ...that you must embrace the pain to forgive. The thought of the demise of my family structure eventually demanded me to face the pain of this change. My little family unit of 3 went through a devastating metamorphosis nearly a decade ago. It was challenging to realize the ending of my marriage, consider my daughter, and impact her life as the blows to this union of 3 dreamily yet dreadfully came without time to breathe or even catch my breath, it seemed. All the while, meditating on my little world of family, routine, and expectation, under construction with all required permits, but things came to a complete stop.

Since being professionally removed from the corporate world, I juggled full-time mommy duties and grinding to get my consulting firm and freelance work off the ground.

I endured weeks of drowning in the imaginary and unproductive practice of self-sabotaging thoughts about the demise of my quaint, happily ever after. I had a lot on my plate. But, unfortunately, nothing appeared to be nearing the point of completion. And then my nightingale, Jill Scott, came out with a new album. I swear this woman… Every album of hers, tailored to my life journey, speaks to me powerfully and deep within my soul. When I hear her songs, I wonder how I can put my experience into such moving words as she does, but hey, that's her gift to me and the world, right?!

"But when I wake up,
And one day I will do it,

I have let you go

And everything I went through was beautiful.

I have let you go

And everything I went through was beautiful.

Maybe I, right now, can't see the forest for the trees.

But I will wake up, and everything I went through would be
beautiful".

"But these words to "When I wake up" flipped the switch for me and started me on a profound and transformative journey towards forgiveness, specifically forgiveness of myself for the decisions that were staring me in the face. Jill's words help me to wake up from this nightmare and get myself together. My daughter had only the slimmest ideas of what was going on with her mom and dad. The most she would witness is a fuss or argument here or there and twice when we lived separately but never forgetting our family ties and not the dissolution of her parent's marriage. At least that's what I'd hoped. A sweet, charming family was my daughter's reality at the time, and she needed me to wake up from this stagnate disposition and prepare for this transformation. I felt that Jill's song was my confirmation that things would be ok and beautiful when I wake up. Lord knows I had to play that song every time I entered my car. It was a self-designed behavioral management strategy where repeated exposure to a stimulus would reinforce that behavioral response predicted to reoccur based on a sufficient payoff. (those who know me know that I always bring it back to education. Lol).

Preparation for the death of my family? Preparation for the scariest transition I've ever experienced in life was worse than preparing for the LSAT or any other challenging test of your applications of the life skills presented in class thus far. The newfound set of circumstances set up in my mind was nearly impossible to examine or recognize in its entirety. I could only catch glimpses here and there, nothing substantial. As I continued to emerge from this dream, I would feel as though I was given only one or two pieces of the picture simultaneously and waited for the next opportunity to land a corner puzzle piece. If only to espy a mere glimpse of my transformation. Decidedly, I had to get out of my head and grasp the impact of what was to come. Getting out of my head meant scheduling my sobbing for smaller intervals of time and much later in the day. Often moments after bedtime triggered a good cry. Erasing tasks from to-do lists became the priority. I took to actualizing positive outcomes for this inevitable brokenness. Visualizing the positive became more manageable once my daughter returned home. As the weeks went on, I worried about how my marriage's demise would impact my daughter. I calculated that my daughter would be better off with two happy, separate parents that could select more suitable partners.

Years ago, as a senior in college, I mentored some women looking to get off public assistance and back into the workplace. One of the first things I impressed upon the women was that they needed to see the change that they desired for their life. As one of these groups of women facilitators, I stressed to them the need to visualize their success and the benefit of writing it down for daily triggers to get on the job of 'gettin her done.' The goal is to be zealous and visualize their dreams in color and adamantly specify the details to their objectives.

And with the same unique force, as a thoroughbred horse bolting from the starting gate when the gun snaps, the practice to visualize the happy ending solidified. As the days went on, I wrote positive thoughts in every place I could find, on my iPhone, iPad, in my journal, and in every space, I could doodle the positive visualizations to propel me forward. Preparing for my daughter's return and the new path on my yellow brick road had me fueled to seek the new beginnings that were bound to be on the horizon.

By the time my daughter returned home, positive visualization on this matter was my first name and a daily mantra ushering me through each day. So much so, when finally speaking to her about the coming change,

I explained that these things happen at times, but both of her parents were still great people, just not right for each other as husband and wife. I wanted her to know that it's ok to love us both and that we would always be her parents and love her just the same, if not more.

The act of positive visualization also consisted of me praying God would keep us both as effective co-parents. And that my daughter would be a better individual despite our choices. Positive thoughts and visualizations of positive experiences provided the countenance for the peregrinations ahead.

"You should never view your challenges as a disadvantage. Instead, it's important for you to understand that your experience facing and overcoming adversity is one of your biggest advantages," said during the 2016 City College of New York commencement speech.

Resilience is the ability to be tough, to have a coping ability that allows you to recoup when exhausted or depleted. I have heard that Sistahs (African American Women for those of you still learning) have this indelible characteristic of resilience and an unconquerable soul. So, of course, you know...I have experienced women of African descent's phenomenal success on a large scale, particularly in marriage, professional, and family success. I reflected on my life and how I had all the ingredients for a successful life and family. I came from a two-parent home. My grandparents were still married, and those who weren't were widowed or remarried for decades. And I thought to myself, what happened with my family and me? If divorce is where this is heading, how in the hell would I be the least bit successful in this next endeavor? How do I survive this; how do I curate a suitable life out of a divorce. This territory is unknown to me. I don't have any examples of "how to recoup from divorce" in my circles. Thankfully, my community supported me while I tried to pick up my life and family.

How would I learn to cope with my marriage falling apart, my daughter's impression of her parents splitting, and how our decision to separate impacted her emotional lability in her relationships both as a child and adult?

I anxiously considered my daughter's interpretation of events manifesting in her life.

Just these thoughts alone snuggly embraced me continually throughout the morning, noonday and night. Night after night, suspended over my side of the bed and deeply disturbed by my set of circumstances, I was furious at him, at myself for allowing things to get here. I thought, "Well, God, I have tried everything, and he has the nerve to be recalcitrant about our marriage, whether the resolution or dissolution of it all; what else do I do but go my own way?."

One evening in May, on the way home from the store, I was amazed at the super moon and how it showed so bright that night, and for that moment, I wasn't in that space of "WTF is happening to my life," my marriage, my family?! While admiring the beauty of the moon, I became instantly and astutely aware of how this strange, new, and perpetual sting lassoed around my heart and soul seemed to loosen its grip and allow me to breathe without the feel of duress. As a young girl, my mother nurtured the love of astrology and the grandeur of celestial bodies, which rubbed off on me but only in the sense of wonderment. I remembered being amazed by the cyclical nature of the moon, planets, and constellations. But I didn't get the same excitement from the knowledge of the night skyline creeping up in the rearview. Late nights and early mornings no longer held the same sentiment as they once did. Instead, these hours proved to be exhaustingly haunting. I didn't await the fall of the sun into the southern hemisphere, and the bright shine of the moon as darkness befell the earth any longer. But come August 3rd of 2012, with the warm rays of the sun cradling my face and locs as I lay in the bed that early morning proved to be the outlay of a brand new day, a brand new journey. One would usher in work on a renovated map of coping with this notion of divorce that confiscated my life. Knowing me the way I do…, in no way was I ready for some kind of smooth transitioning to embrace a palpable venture into the future.

Believe it or not, visualization is similar to the prewriting phase in writing. It's creating thoughts and setting a paradigm for future writing, connecting ideas, and making sense of your vision. My dreams of getting through this unfortunate set of events in my personal life, while intact and with an 'emotionally whole' daughter, would not become a reality without some perspective to help leverage this heavy load to a more manageable position. Now, it is not as easy as it sounds. But instead, it was genuinely spiritual when I woke up to the rest of my life. Once I achieved a more positive perspective, I still had a lot of work to do. And now was the time to map out the same strategy I taught in my senior year in college...see yourself successful in life no matter the lemons sent your way. Albeit, the stratagem of life is to study but not too long, right?! That piece of advice is directly from my father.

My community was the foothold I needed to focus on to get my footing on the matter. These women were my saving grace when I had no idea where to turn or what would be my next step. Afraid of missing an opportunity, fearful of what my circumstances mean for me now, and most fearful of not developing a more desirable set of experiences, it was my community of support that relieved a portion of already bottled up fear. The machinations involved would astound my thoughts about the future, mostly since I was front and center at this feature. Simultaneously, I endured some purging in my social circles, which is a later story to explore. But my most pressing issue required a community of support and encouragement to get me to the other side of this bridge to a different life. And just like that, before I could plan, my circle was planning to get me over this obstacle. Providing options for me to get out of such a stressful circumstance, my circle of support came through for me. Everyone remembers the famous statement about people in your life, and I will say that these ladies are definitely in my life for a reason and not just a season.

As home life became hectic, it was time for my daughter's annual summer trip. It was vital for me to stay busy outside of the home, work my consulting business, and organize my affairs. The first week of August arrived, and my circle of sisters took me in to help with my transition. Of course, my circle of support extended back home to Alabama, where even my best friend traveled to spend a week with me to ensure I was ok. Honestly, my girls were the best thing for me outside of God, meditation, and busywork. As I reflect on this time, my girls were indeed the foundation that kept me afloat. Their love, encouragement, and support kept me resilient during my family's transition.

A year before this all began to unfold, I had left the corporate world to give my daughter more support and start my educational consulting firm. From August to October, I moved in with a sister-friend until I found a place for my daughter and me. If it weren't for them, I can't imagine how I would have made it through attorneys' research, the number of court visits to file paperwork, the court date, moving out, situating my daughter upon returning home, and moving into my place. Newly single after 15 years and raising a daughter *with love, care, and understanding,* coupled with her family's previous dynamics, was a terrifying experience for me. Even with the support of my circle of sister-friends and family, I continued to feel horrible about the predicament I found myself in. Before I finally left home, he would make grand gestures of remorse, asking for me to forgive him and come back to love; each time I looked at the family photos in my phone and my wallet, I sobbed like a baby because I was the one who filed for divorce at the end of the day. And if it weren't for my circle of sisters, my community, my squad, I am not sure that I would have recovered from this setback. Instead, my community helped me to grow through this circumstance.

"Dreams are lovely. But they are just dreams. Fleeting, ephemeral, pretty. But dreams do not come true just because you dream them. It's hard work that makes things happen. It's hard work that creates change." — Shonda Rhimes.

I had a dream. I thought it was a lovely dream. As a young girl, I had a great marriage vision, such as in A Table for Two. Once I got married, I had plans of a beautiful marriage while raising our children to be great conscientious, confident, and compassionate people in this world. I had visions of being an empty-nester and seeing the world, living at the beach, and walking naked with my man through the house. And I knew that I'd put in the hard work on this dream well before treading in the waters of infidelity and divorce.

We were pressing forward. Transitioning to single and divorced life was by no means easy, smooth, or a walk in the park. I could still feel the sting of his words that day. I could even see my dreams of the future melting away. So I continued to hurt and not understand why or how I allowed this to happen to me. After all, I'm a planner; I try to anticipate what happens next; I try to have a backup plan. But this seemed to be different because I got married with the adamancy of no divorce or my family's demise. And here I was! Time went on for my daughter and me;

we finally moved into our place and began to walk the path set before us, *Two Belles in the City*.

We packed up our positive perspective and moved right on to DC. Here was Karma again, as Sacajawea's baby girl following her mom into another adventure, a new world to us. We managed to securely transport gratefulness and fortitude straight from Maryland to NE DC in addition to our full view. And though I couldn't see all of the pieces of the puzzle, I knew things would come together if we just kept pressing forward.

The end of the year brought the finalization of my divorce and a 'successful survival' of sorts. I had secured housing and other essentials to make our transition smoother. But the sting of failure outweighed any sense of accomplishment. I was often numb from the sting but depressed about the dreams shattered by the decision to leave. I didn't grow up in a home where couples irrevocably disagreed or reached an impasse pushing the other to go permanently. I saw couples work through issues such as this, if not more minor issues, than infidelity. After six months of therapy, prayer, and even medication, I realized that what I'd understood to be the foundation of the relationships I grew up knowing was not the prescription for me. At least that's how I felt when he posed the notion of what makes me better than other women that had experienced their husband's infidelity?'. As I reflected on his provocation, later on, I wept as I came to understand the sacrifices made by women to keep their families intact. Insanity nearly drowned me as I questioned whether I could do it also, keep my family intact and go on with life as initially planned. Should I remain in this marriage for several more years to keep our family together until she graduates from secondary school? I kept telling myself that I was doing what was right in terms of my sanity, my daughter's view of her mother as it related to men, and for us together in this new family of sorts. However, I could see her disappointment in me and my decision to leave the marriage in my daughter's eyes. I could empathize with the pain she felt when I would inquire about how she felt, and typically, her response was a shrug of her shoulders or the aversion of her eyes when I'd asked if she'd need to speak with someone about her feelings.

I chose to determine the exemplar needed for my little girl, my Ace, was to keep looking forward. Keep moving towards the goal. Map and walk out the plan. Being the spiritual woman I am, I invoked God to guide me all during this process. Daily, before the middle school drop-offs at St. Augustine, we prayed together and asked for guidance, protection, and discernment because I was moving forward. What did I know about raising our daughter in a single-parent home? This thing called divorce was uncharted territory, and though I wasn't a pioneer on the matter, I was indeed a foreigner, someone not of this particular world—all in all, I was pressing on.

One Saturday, my friend called me to chat, and I expressed that I felt like I was failing at life. The most important thing to me was the success of my family. In my eyes, we were nowhere near the midline of progress, let alone close to success. This blow took more than just my breath away; it knocked me off of my feet, and I realized that it would be longer than usual to catch my second wind. How could I regroup and keep moving forward or do I regroup and ship out? She mentioned that she was at a loss for words in that I appeared to be handling everything with unbelievable grace. It was at that moment when I realized that my perspective on the world was about to change. Acknowledging this distraught course of affairs was a learning experience and not a failure to die by.

Traveling down Route One in Virginia to DC, I had to break the news to my Ace that her parents would be getting a divorce. It was a sticky issue, discussing this with her. I wanted to speak to her about the situation without lying to her about what happened. A grimy impetus and not the most honorable thing a daughter should understand about her dad, I decided to inform her with a motherly and caring touch of the unfortunate events of love between two people. I noticed her eyes set on mine for what felt like an infinite amount of time. I could feel her dark brown eyes pierce my soul with a sound only my heart could hear. This family was her tiny nucleus of the world, and who was Mom to go and just stomp it all up? Until this day, I can feel my daughter's bewilderment as I spoke those words to her. She asked me why we decided to divorce, and I told her plainly that sometimes two people who love each other can fall in love with someone else (which is correct but socially unacceptable for married couples). I attempted to present a more tolerable perspective of this calamity causing a mess of everything. Little did she know how her positive outlook was critical to the entire plan to thrive being successful. Positive perspective and pressing forward created a gear shift for me!

In the second year of being fully self-employed, newly divorced, with a small child in tow, I needed to hold tight to a different perspective! I was self-employed with at-risk clients or cheap attorneys wanting free work; my income perspective also shifted. It was back into the workforce as an employee. I'd have to turn my consulting firm into a side hustle. Can you imagine the bummer? But what can you do when you're starting over in Washington, DC, with a small child in tow? Get a regular paying job and preferably in an area in which I am proficient. So while sending out student enrollment packets for clients, I also inquired about available positions because babies must eat, right?! The plan was to keep moving forward despite the obstacles. Get up, sis, and keep going. And with grace, we did just that...kept going, kept smiling, kept laughing, kept learning, and kept loving her, life, and myself. As we continued to keep moving forward in our new life, my journaling picked up significantly, where previously I would have a journal for at least a year; I had purchased at least three journals filled by the end of the year. There were words and thoughts to write about, questions that I needed to ponder and get an answer to, and scenarios that required me to play out before they transpired. With each completed journal, I'd take a weekend to ponder on that time and how I could improve and then look to start the next chapter of my life. After doing this for about nine months, I could chart this journey for us and, more specifically, self-reflect for perspective.

Very significant progress on co-parenting efforts with my ex-husband proved to be critical in the healthy development of our daughter. The first two years after the breakup resembled the same time in Obama's quest to get the ACA passed in the senate. But each time we were able to speak civilly with each other, I reminded him how important it was for us to work on our relationship concerning our daughter. She deserves to see her parents respect one another, continue to enjoy the same company, not allow the family members not to feel like family, appear irreconcilable, and most importantly, see her father treat her mother well. I demanded these be critical to our co-parenting formula. There would continue to be a few blowout arguments sprinkled throughout the year. We went from each conversation ending in a fight to about once a quarter—another self-reflection from journal writing. So, I mentioned some of the things I had observed in our previous conversations. Then we'd have a long discussion about those findings and end in an argument about the whole thing, diagnosis, and prognosis. By the time she started college, she had understood the importance of her parents' relationship to her conditioning. If I am one of her role models, I wanted to show a practical and strategic demand for respect as an adult woman/mother, and she needed to keep it moving and still rely on family support. I also wanted her to know that you can always choose family even when the ties that bind appear broken. Our co-parenting relationship was also crucial. As her first teacher, I also strived to see the contradiction of African American Men and Women who can't get along,

Black Love is hard, or friendships can't evolve. It was a parallel journey at times...co-parenting.

Though parenting is a lifelong journey, I'd come to realize a few things about this transition. The first is that sometimes things fall apart only to come together if you keep moving forward. Secondly, my accomplishments proved that I can always make lemonade even when it seems you don't have all of the ingredients. Looking back, I can see the pearls of wisdom and character-building sparked from this situation. Finally, as a Black woman and a Black mother to a daughter, I have grown as an individual and someone worth forgiving.

"But when I wake up

Everything I went through would be beautiful."

Good Friends to Build the Village

"Surround yourself with only people who are going to lift you higher."
– Oprah Winfrey

In a blue tank top bikini, lying on the beach, with my long legs stretched out on the blanket, journal, and pen in hand while Jill is playing. I began to scribble on the parchment-like paper; the voice in my head was shouting idea after idea. It was a great idea to take off on a road trip with her and spend some mother-daughter time outside our everyday routine. However, not too long after the divorce was final, I feared the journey would damage our relationship, and it's challenging to repair. So we finally shared a spring break again, and I decided that we should make a go of it and head out to the beach—a place we both love very much. I quietly listened to the waves rolling into the shore and smiled as I watched Karma, who was still a young girl, was sitting smack in the middle of her fort while she built a castle. As I smiled at how amused she found herself, I took another look at the scene she'd engineered. Karma quickly staked out her section of the beach, laid down the line of protection, and began to build out her vision. It appeared as though her small world had been situated for a prosperous future. The land was vacant, and the view was breathtaking and serene. She made a few small castles on her plot of white sandy beach but rendered helpless to giant waves hitting the shore. Her long legs spiritedly running towards the ocean with her locs snappily bouncing behind her. I wistfully reminisced on the ability to be carefree and run into the crashing waves just as she did that day.

Watching her bright and silly giggle just like she did when she was three, I smiled as I waited for Karma to eventually find a shell and bring it to me to behold its majesty. It resembled the home of a mollusk which I thought was very interesting to be so close to the shoreline. Being a "true Southern Belle," of course, I immediately thought, "Was there a pearl inside?" That has always been my silent wish when at the beach, finding my pearl. Still journaling about this moment, I considered the clam, the symbiotic relationship with nacre, and *all* of my *everything*. So as an ambitious sister determined to make better decisions and apply some of my instruction, I realized the several passions in my life that I find myself protecting. Simultaneously, it matures, and the instances where I may 'catch a kink,' I'd have to regroup and learn the lesson quickly. As a result of this slight obsession and the presence of my smart and beautiful daughter, I have a few pearls to certify my status!

Interestingly all of my passions include changing the world, leaving the world better for my little one. There'd even be times when I would hear Karma's voice in my head, "You should do it!!" And, of course, she was/is right to think that about her mom. But, many times, the notion of writing down new ideas would only record the date the idea would begin to die due to those self-sabotaging thoughts of "lack of… " lack of time and access. So I figured that I'd change my perspective on the results of my situations or current circumstances, which helped me understand my pearls along my journey. Pearls of insight, integrity, and innovation are all intertwined with protecting what is precious. Pearls of wisdom bursting from my strength and my resilience and, most importantly, using the lesson as an opportunity to sparkle. In my terminology, Sparkle is the acknowledgment of the lesson learned, embracing how to apply the new info and use it for improvement, the complete cycle of self-assessment. And after reviewing my journals, I mapped how I created pearls when my dream job just plopped in my lap and my circle that helped usher me into my greatness.

In 2012, Aimee Mussington, my roommate from Undergrad and the Director of Student Support Services, gave me a call after viewing my online presence as a special educator. Aimee was my second roommate in undergraduate school. Tall, slim with smooth, dark-skinned, and quick common-sense quibbles as it related to real-life scenarios, Aimee found me on social media and didn't hesitate to send a homing pigeon my way for her professional educational needs. When we lived together, I was intrigued by her response to what would later be described as 'stanning' nowadays. Smart guys were enchanted with her and appeared to be quite aware that only young men with their act together would get the time of day from her. Aimee didn't waiver when it came to her position on dating, and now she was about to get married while improving her school system's approach to students with disabilities.

At this time, I transitioned out of the classroom and into academic administration, policy, and law, and interestingly enough, professional development was on my horizon. After our working conference, it became apparent the size of the project. The proposal was to provide consulting on the school district's effectiveness related to children with special needs. And my deliverables were to create a manual and facilitate a week-long professional development conference to train the district's most significant stakeholders, ranging from teachers, administrators, and parents, on best practices for this school community. At first glance, this appeared to be a daunting task, but it required an unprecedented commitment level.

This commitment required setting priorities both personally and professionally to push my proclivities of organization and focus to the extent that allowed me to address matters thoroughly. Simultaneously, they were manageable and strategically planned goals in multiple areas of my life. This project built up my confidence as a skilled special education educator, a consummate professional, and a fierce advocate for those who need protection the most. A professional educational conference was held on the beautiful island of Saint Maarten of the Netherlands Antilles to train the educational stakeholders within the Ministry of Education. This wonderful, life-changing experience would be one of my three mothers of pearls.

Though I juggled being a mom, along with establishing my dream of an educational firm, family, and some marital issues, to say I'd become distracted would be an understatement. I began to lose my grasp on the value of time management of the task list for this critical project. Of course, the confluence of each of these situations led me to journal more which brought a time of reflection. Here I was sixty days before my international educational conference in St. Maarten and simultaneously strategizing how to reorganize my life. And according to the 2018 State of Women-owned Business report, "There are 2.4 million African American women-owned businesses in 2018, most owned by women 35 to 54. According to the Federal Reserve, black women are the only racial or ethnic group with more business ownership than their male peers."

Being a part of this number, I figured the appropriate application of my advice on perspective and self-assessment was critical to my situation. With so many hits to my strategic plan, the adverse effects took away chunks of my confidence. My self-confidence in this journey was Mandatory! It was essential to be humble but more critical for me to cultivate the formation of this pearl. The cultivation of this pearl was not just about the educational conference but more about me rising to the occasion of acknowledging the next level of my career. This opportunity would help solidify me as an expert on special education, which I marketed to the public.

A business strategy learned directly from my now ex-husband was to research my product and my audience's relationship to the product. Regardless of my craft, he expressed the importance of developing insight into how my product or service would meet customers' needs. And to keep my expectations optimistic but realistic. Research and in-depth knowledge of my services, the audience, and the relationship between the two factions can synthesize an increase in my confidence and the confidence of others that benefit from collaborating with me.

Speaking of him… it was the gift of his most important lesson that was the most life-changing. Like a bull in a China shop, as the old saying goes, this ball of confusion came into our lives, shaking the very foundations of my perspective on love, life, and family, along with shattering a couple of cornerstones of our relationship. Adultery is a tricky topic to consider and discuss, especially with the spouse that has committed such a transgression. And believe me when I say to you that we had our share of discussions regarding this topic. As I mentioned earlier, I was consumed with the notion of this affair. It seemed I cried for days and days while he was at work and Karma at school, then again later at night while lying next to him until morning.

Sometimes clients who experience a partner's infidelity meet the criteria for posttraumatic stress disorder (PTSD), says Gabrielle Usatynski, a licensed professional counselor (LPC) and founder of Power Couples Counseling in Boulder and Louisville, Colorado. Lindsey Phillips (*lindseynphillips.com*) in Counseling Today, A Publication of the American Counseling Association, April 1, 2020. This explanation clearly defined what I was experiencing and what I would call PTSD from acknowledging his betrayal! I experienced triggers, flashbacks, hypervigilance, avoidance behavior, and manifestations related to the knowledge about his affair and everything related to it. Adultery and the notion of its interjection in our marriage set me back royally. In the middle of the climb to be a power couple in the DC Metropolitan area, he and I now have to contend with the demise of our hard work so far.

As the days passed, I realized that as a wife and a black woman raised in a two-parent home who married a man from a two-parent home, I now had to consider that my family failed to meet at least the benchmark of our parents' marriages. Notwithstanding that I had a substantial consulting project on the table with big dollars associated with its finalization, I had to regroup and do it by yesterday's arrival. I remember reading many different articles on marital issues and how to cope with the trauma. The most influential advice I received was to focus on what you can control and occupy yourself when you may catch yourself having flashbacks of the transgression. Luckily, our neighborhood had a community preschool, and they required a lead teacher, so I applied and got the job. It was only 5 hours a day and just enough time to earn some money, keep my mind busy simultaneously making space to focus on the consulting project with St. Maarten.

The building reminds you of the Keebler House from the outside, with wood paneling on windows placed around an octagon-shaped frame nestled in the community's center. It was surrounded by tall trees with a park on the left-hand side. The perfect thing about the school's placement over and above the central location in the neighborhood was that the gym was cater-corner to pre-K. It's here, at Cornerstone, that I met Nathaly, a bright, savvy, and saucy young lady from Columbia. After leaving the firm downtown, it was great to meet her because we had some things in common, educating small children and the conjoined enjoyment of "girl time." Not only did we work together at the preschool, but we were gym buddies, exchanged recipes, discussed career and family goals, and went out for Tequila a few times, and this list is not exhaustive. Nathaly lived in the neighborhood, just a block up from my building, with the school and gym in the middle of our homes, so it worked well for our friendship. Still out of sync with the project's timeline and nowhere in the headspace to focus on it, Nathaly's friendship helped get me where I needed to get my act together.

It was great to have another teacher within the classroom to assist with the day's schedule. Not that I couldn't handle it, but an extra set of productive hands are always welcomed in an efficient preschool classroom. The class composition was primarily boys and two girls, ages 3.5-5 years of age, and Nathaly was my teacher's assistant. During planning time, she'd asked questions about my teaching and classroom management strategies which prompted me to be serious about these instances and equip her with practical tools to use within the classroom. I would review lessons and create plans that encompassed moments of incidental teaching. It was just what I needed to kick start my brain to focus on the nuances of educating children, which would simultaneously get my mind on the St. Maarten project.

One day after work, we discussed a student who always gave us some trouble during transition times (bathroom, snack, prayer, lunch, and nap). On this particular day, our favorite student, let's call him Thomas, began to cry loudly during our transition to the restroom. We had been intermittently intervening in his behavior with the most limited interaction, not indirectly reinforcing the behavior needing replacement. His behaviors kept him near the teacher during transitions but not haphazardly but more of a strategic approach to mitigating any triggers for inappropriate behaviors. During the potty time, Thomas would find a way to express his displeasure with how he figured his will should strongly influence this transition. I noticed how he became immediately distracted by others in the classroom during the lineup. Immediately I made him the line leader and the bathroom monitor (who was standing right by the door to ensure they washed their hands) for his peers. He didn't cry during that transition, and after snacking, he was so happy with himself that we didn't have to encourage him to go to sleep. After that episode, Nathaly and I hung pretty tight. She studied under the tutelage of a well-known psychologist in Columbia, her mother. Nathaly was a no-nonsense woman with a slender frame, dirty blonde hair, and newly married while trying to acclimate to American life. Her friendship gave me a new perspective on my immediate issues, aspects of personality, and human behavior. Our friendship kept me in the driver's seat and brave enough to figure out this mess.

Soul Sisters that summer of 2012 and with Nathaly's encouragement, her timely outings to let down our rolling curls (both of us had shoulder-length hair with bouncing curls) it was a bond I'd cherish for a lifetime. Then finally, I cleared the infidelity fog and got back to what was familiar...work. We both recognized that my first step was to get organized. Organization of my resources both for the project, the terms of engagement agreement, the information I'd need for the divorce proceedings, and Karma. And though me and Karma's dad had not worked out anything between us except that one of us would be sleeping on the couch, things were still all over the place. There would be arguments, name-calling, and just unbridled tension when we were at home together. And on those days, the contention was as thick as the government cheese in the long grey rectangle box that made the best cheese sandwiches. LOL.

Being in my community and my friend was the impetus to our initial bond of educating children. Our common interests outside of the classroom encouraged my love of sharing my skills with others to benefit the welfare of children. Both of us were raising daughters to be emotionally healthy young women. However, Nathaly had had her fair share of bad experiences with people she trusted. She was a recent newlywed and free from marital issues, but she too was hoping to find a friendship. Having a previous run-in situation as an Au Pair, she really enjoyed caring for children and desired to make a living from her passion. As an educator, most of my peers work with older students, and to have a peer with similar educational interests was a delight I treasured as a professional. She could and often would create a whole world out of clay that mesmerized even the oldest child. Nathaly is a natural-born creative, and this quality paid off in our classroom. And her perspective on child development was fresh, and she could grasp the connection between the environment and behavior. As an educator with an extensive background in child development and behavior analysis, our relationship with the students in the classroom and the study of our student's development was critical to our discussions and problem solving, even for the Special Education Conference in St. Maarten.

So as the project timeline continued to approach the date of the deliverable, I had to roll with the punches and juggle my responsibilities with style and grace. ....because now my perspective was all about the hustle. I learned that rolling with the punches is about understanding that defense is just as crucial as your offense. Having Nathaly in my corner during this time influenced my perspective on my situation. It was critical to creating adaptable and effective strategies when planning the outlay of the conference and one of my most important transitions. Forbes magazine describes adaptability as "… people, teams, and organizations to adapt to changes in their environments, stay relevant and avoid obsolescence is the defining characteristic between success and failure, growth and stagnation, business and bankruptcy". *Forbes.com September 3, 2015.*

Because adaptation in business requires one to learn from others, finding mentors who could guide my product and services became another priority. I managed to form a mentoring relationship with an Educational Consultant in Alexandria, Va., and a small business attorney in DC. These relationships allowed me to elevate my brand and level of business acumen in the DMV educational arena. Both mentors guided me along the process as I adapted the services I'd provide because my client's needs had changed. By October 15 of that year, I presented my deliverables. The contract was approved, the retainer paid, travel and lodge arrangements finalized, and last but not least, I had purchased my wardrobe for the trip.

It was about 1:30 pm that day, and my heart began to palpitate because as I finalized the documents for the electronic transfer, it was clear that I was one step closer to my dream. I didn't know any of my friends or colleagues that had this experience, so I was pretty proud of myself and this accomplishment. The document transfer was complete! I called up Nathaly for our daily gym session. Stoked about the current milestone, I ran to the bedroom closet to pull out my gym clothes. Slipping on my shorts and sports bra, I quickly stuffed my locs in a scrunci and slid my feet inside my Auburn University colored New Balance to hit the street and celebrate the news with a run on the treadmill. The best thing about our friendship was our shared interest: education and children, healthy living along with music and Tequila. And of course, we worked out and went out later that day to celebrate in our favorite style: music, laughs, and drinks. Downtown DC at Recessions was our party destination. We met up with some legal friends who sent an invite earlier in the day to come and party with Karaoke to turn up!

That night, I celebrated with many of my peers, and it felt awesome to see the fruits of my labor, at least the initial buds coming up. The next day my visit to the gym was much later in the day, of course. Just because I transferred over the documents, I still had to prepare for the conference later in the month; I still had some work to do before my flight left Reagan National Airport. I checked the time on my Blackberry and realized Karma and her dad were not expected home any time soon, so I took to the quietness of my home as an opportunity to journal and reflect on this entire season and what I've learned about myself. I hopped out of the shower, put on a comfortable tee shirt, and made myself some coffee while I got out my journal, pen, and thoughts.

I earned several pearls on this professional journey that coincided with the demise of my marriage. One of the pearls I most admire was the one that captured my sheer courage to tackle such a demand all the while I was going through a divorce after 12.5 years of marriage to my college sweetheart. I can remember like it was yesterday when I discovered his indiscretion and the day I filed for divorce because of it. Writing my first resource manual was something that I figured I get around to much later in life. When working for the law firm or even in my classrooms, I always created a resource manual with all critical information and clear flow charts for routine procedures. Again this project was designed specifically for me, but it took courage to accomplish it.

The most glaring aspect of my personality, my ability to keep going even when it seemed that all of the investment of time and effort, and bandwidth I'd given to the masonry of my future, was the sustaining fuel of my perseverance. There was a sincere yearning to see the light at the end of the tunnel. I needed to see the sun emerge from behind the clouds, and this was the secret my soul cradled while I cried myself to sleep. The picture of people only seeing the duck gliding above the water, and they have no clue as to his feet fluttering frantically underneath. Once I truly accepted the notion that this would be an exciting opportunity, I couldn't wait another minute to create a bucket list and set out to live my best life. From leaving a legacy in print to traveling the world to tell my story, I have been slowly checking items off my list.

But given my will to persevere, where would I be if I didn't have my community? Nevertheless, my colleagues and my personal friends were integral in my *ease down the road* to find my way home. God always has a plan, right? Unbeknownst to my colleague, Aimee, it was this professional opportunity that I needed to keep my perspective and not become debilitating and consumed with the affair. There were months of research completed and meetings with colleagues like Ed Galiber, M.Ed., and Roxanne Neloms, Esq. and Tilman Gerald, Esq. on the best approach to achieving the business contracts and formatting the presentations for the conference. These bastions of educational rights within DC are just a few great examples of a community lifting their own to a higher plane. I worked with each of them in different aspects of the project, from the contracting, educational formatting of the conference, and compliance issues that would need to be addressed. Having their confidence and witnessing their pouring into me included more than just professional guidance with the conference and increasing my business acumen. I can genuinely say these three were more than willing to take a chance on my brand of education and me. Each colleague continues to support me professionally by pouring into my dreams regularly.

Part III

Sparkle

The kind of beauty I want most is the hard-to-get
kind that comes from within - strength, courage,
dignity.--Ruby Dee

Femininity

Mary Alston Sledge was one of the first women in my bloodline that forged a love of family, self-pride, and dignity. She exemplified ladyhood, femininity, and strength. My grandmother was a kind, reserved, and giving woman, the matriarch of the Sledge Family, also known as Ms. May on West Patton Avenue. Smooth and supple mocha skin, high cheekbones, bright smile with an inconspicuously placed gold cap on her tooth just inside the crease of her lip that you only caught a glimpse of if she gave a hearty smile, Grandma wore print 1960's style dresses, cinched in the waist with an A-line train with the espadrille slides. Ms. Mary knew a good drink when she had one. The only woman I didn't shy away from because she smoked or had an inconspicuous gold tooth, she was a little bit feisty, conveniently sassy, and her home girls' homegirl. Ms. Mary ran a tight ship at 332, whether preparing a meal or prepping the house for her Tuesday night Pokeno game. As my first babysitter, she introduced me to the love of books, femininity (as it relates to demeanor, fashion, and self-care management in the form of regular Mani and Pedi's with salmon-colored nail polish), the value of girlfriends, the familial fellowship at the dining table, generational adventures, and the love of the bond that tradition creates. Through ritual and dignity, these demonstrations of love were Ms. Mary's *Sparkle* even though she encountered her challenges on her journey.

Being an only child and seemingly an orphan because her mother passed away when she was in grade school, the family bond was essential to her very being. Ms. Mary stressed that I should never have just one child because they'd always feel alone in the world. I knew this sentiment came from her feelings of disconnect. She created traditions among her brood and showed the importance of a family's rhythm shown through her cooking, sewing, and even rearing children. And for 332 West Patton Avenue, breakfast time was her first dance routine. Every morning at Grandma's house, as I lay in the bed, the sunbeams forcibly walked across the floor of the room to my eyelids; I could smell coffee brewing, pots and pans clamoring, and the local channel 12 news announcing the weather for the day.

As a babe of the South, brewing coffee with sizzling sausage patties is an undeniably luring smell. The Folgers coffee brewing would waft through the air of the house and tickle everyone's nose as a gentle alarm to the little women of the house to get up and come help put breakfast on the table. For the little women of the house, the tickling scent of coffee was a light touch that indicated Grandma needed our help to set the table and get everyone else up when breakfast was nearly on the table. Cooking was only one of the ways that she'd show love. Her love for feeding her family was twofold and just as strong as her love for tradition, custom, and the routine show of love through communion. Cooking was her way of making a house a home, and it was her language of love for the girls in the home. It was a sacredly communal time for the household. An intricate and ritualistic dance between the women and the men of the house, where the women prepared the food while the men got ready for their day, was the breakfast dance. Preparing meals and serving her family was how Ms. Mary loved her family. It was a yeoman's work on her hands and her feet as she stood to cook and clean and drenched her hands in harsh chemicals and running several times a day, all for the love of the family she built. But in loving others, she was keen on loving herself, and both her love for family and herself were traditions that she passed on to her Daughters' Sledge.

Any woman that has managed a household, whether single or in the construction of a family, knows that it takes work and skill to do it effectively. Cooking for the family takes a lot of time management, organization, discipline, and efficiency. Nevertheless, Grandma had found the rhythm that allowed her to engage the task successfully, seemingly without much thought. Breakfast, my favorite meal, would always have something different: a new addition or particular swap out that kept breakfast enjoyable like poached eggs, or salmon croquette with potatoes, or souse meat and grits. The downside to this show of love was the mornings of rinsing and drying dishes to set the table and washing dishes after the meals were over. Me, myself, I hated washing dishes! Early on, I hadn't figured out how to combat the harshness of the water and soapy water on my hands. The many hangnails, split cuticles, splitting nails, and dry skin drove me crazy. As a child, I'd find myself using my teeth to maintain my hand care which, of course, made things worse. So one morning, after washing dishes and watching Donohue with her and my grandfather, I went to complain to her about my terrible disdain for washing dishes. "Grandma, why couldn't the boys wash the dishes sometimes? My hands are so dry, and my fingernails hurt. I hate it. Please let them do it tomorrow, and Aunt Sonda and I will just get ready as they do." My grandmother chucked with her signature smile that curved to the left with a slight nod of acknowledgment.

Sitting on her navy blue couch in her den (a room that her sons built for her when my grandfather's lung health continued to decline), Grandma motioned for me to get her lotion and nail tools (manicure set) and began to show me a nice workaround to my dilemma. Before this teachable moment, I'd inadvertently noticed that she'd pull this manicure set out and work on her hands for about thirty minutes to an hour, including nail polish selections and scented oils for her fingers. She spoke softly to me about the self-care steps for my hands because, as she saw it, my participation in the intricate dance of her commitment to her love language was not as negotiable as one would think.

It was this day that I noticed my grandmother's hands in more detail. Grandma's hands resembled a landscape of tributaries that flowed from her phalanges towards her tiny feminine wrists. As I eyed the intricacy of her hands, I noticed the delicacy of the care required to keep her hands healthy and prepared for the work they were destined to accomplish as she nurtured her family and demonstrated her love for others. Given her investment in her family, she had a very dignified approach to the care of her hands. Grandmother was particular about being feminine. Her fingers were slender and chocolate with a smooth nail bed with signature half-moons. Her favorite nail color was a soft pink or salmon color that pronounced the essence of femininity that she exuded even when wearing one of her favorite sixties house dress with wedge espadrilles. As she demonstrated how I should give myself a manicure to address my 'dishwashing hands,' this was one of my grandma's first self-care lessons. And because of this lesson from my best friend, manicures are something I practice to this day. Therefore, I felt it necessary to pass this self-care lesson on to my daughter when she turned ten.

As a nine-year-old girl learning the importance of self-care, I felt like I was becoming a young woman and that this level of care was a part of that process. Our nail care routines, her dignified approach to family, and food prep for the masses that always managed to show up at West Patton were aspects of her femininity founded in her sense of tradition that she learned growing up and as a young woman of a family of 10, including her and my grandfather. As I have grown older, I have been told that my hands resemble her own. My spirit smiles when I hear this notion. All these years since her passing away, I continue to keep her traditions of showing love healthily for family and self-care to my heart and have sought to pass it on to my daughter. As her love language, the tradition impressed upon us to keep the family bonded and embrace love and dignity.

Being a Southern Belle, this sentiment of a familial language of love was reiterated from my mother-in-law, another Southern Belle in her own right, upon marrying my ex-husband. Before we were married, I'd visited my future in-laws via my brother-in-love's introduction for Memorial Day deep down in rural Alabama, the little town of Odena to be exact. Long winding roads, plenty of greenery, nicely spaced ramblers, small farms of corn, greens, and beans were staples of the community markers and added to the notion of quality of love and care to preparing meals for family and friends.

This first meeting was interesting in that I had never dated a guy and met the majority of his close family members in our first meeting and without him due to a business conference. But it didn't stop my future mother-in-love from saying to me that it's essential to learn how to cook her eldest son's favorite meals. So there I was, in her combination-styled kitchen with her trusty cookbook, ingredients to prepare a seven-layer salad. Full of excitement and ready to embrace this relationship with my future husband's mother, I eagerly welcomed the opportunity to embrace this new family's traditions with their love language, which mirrored my own. By the time Tyree and I were married, both my grandmother and his mother's family traditions were fully ingratiated into my being and love language.

The Daughter of Sledge

Pauline represents the resilience of female energy within the maternal side of the family. Aunt Pauline, a very petite woman, dark-skinned, with that signature Sledge smile, firmly held hands with courage. A very petite woman, her voice was one to be acknowledged, and her personality was a show stopper, but her courage was insurmountable. My aunt started out on her own at the age of 16. She spent her young adulthood traveling the northeast and the state of Alabama singing at the local clubs with her brother, Marion Sledge. Dreams of seeing the world allowed her to live an entire life with love and adventure. As the oldest of Mary's daughters, my Aunt Pauline was named after her dad, no middle name with an unyielding and quite demanding spirit the same as him. Growing up in my grandma's house, she was a curious child who maintained this personality trait until the end. She never failed to be in everybody's business. Luckily for me, she was always with a song coming from deep in the gut along with an internal syncopation. Aunt Pauline had her singing group, The Lovettes, who won several contests in the community, which gave her the confidence to take her talent all over the North American continent. Her disregard for fear gave her a lifetime of experience that I could only dream of as a child. She sang with Canadian bands and lived in Buffalo for a couple of years as a performer. However, her travels are what was the most intriguing about her. A talented and dedicated performer, she made her costumes and perfected her makeup and hair.

When we listened to music together, I can remember how we shared that inner ability to pick up the beat in a melody automatically. Aunt Pauline would always have a line from a song relating to our discussion to re-emphasize a point. This little quirk of hers was contagious. Her abilities translated into her intrigue. Whenever she returned to visit grandma's house, everyone was captivated by her charisma, familiarity, and warmth. It kind of reminds me of the feeling when I'd have some warm chocolate cookies. Every time the air whispered her memory, it was my crew and me who would breathlessly announce her arrival.

So fast forward from our hectic days in the tops of the trees scouting out Aunt Pauline's ventures back to West Patton Avenue to me all "grown." A good 22 years at the time, and here I am, acting like "I'm grown," living on the Southside of Birmingham, Alabama, in a cozy condominium. Now down South, your Momma, Big Momma, Grandma, or your Auntie can use this saying when you are between the ages of 18-30 years old. It is a classic social trope that by the time you get 18, you are fully aware that it's a poke at an envied youth that shows you belong to the village. Aunt Pauline was excited about this in that we could do more together and have more intimate conversations with each other. She saw the opportunity to get to know her surrogate children as adults and share her perspective on the ways of the world. This was the beginning of a more intimate friendship with her where we could exchange our influence. Our friendship would later evolve into a very mature relationship where we shared some of our deepest secrets with one another. However, I would find that the little girl perched in the treetops on West Patton was still alive and filled with cheer when I'd see Aunt Pauline come in off the road of one of her many travels when she came to my home some again this time in DC.

I raced that magic blue Volvo from Hyattsville, MD to Union Station, swerving the District's streets to catch her as she stepped off the platform. Usually, she'd drive herself wherever she decided to take flight, but this time she took the train because of her health. As soon as I pulled up, I spotted her laughing and chatting it up with a new set of friends from Amtrak. Never meeting a stranger, we, Daughters of Sledge, are like that in that way, always ready to chat you up if you need it. Before heading to get Karma and some dinner, she noted how she'd arranged to attend a Kenny Loggins concert back in Ohio later that year with one of her newfound buddies. Her visit was about five days, and I was excited to see and share this time with Karma, and with me now that Karma was old enough to experience the same.

Later that night, she and I talked to the wee hours in the morning about life, love, and family. One of the most moving things that we discussed was her experiences with sexual assault.

She achingly spoke of her first encounter with sexual assault as a young girl by a guy she liked but was too shy to approach. She was not prepared for the onslaught of feelings of anger, disappointment, confusion, and terror she would experience because of this encounter. Youth and naiveté got the best of her as she never thought he would betray her genuine interest in him. In Montgomery, Alabama, in the mid-'60s, at least on the West side of town, was the hub for young blacks, with afros, black leather jackets, bell-bottom pants. Pauline was not your regular neighborhood girl; she was a melanated cutie pie and young celebrity in her community. Even as a young girl, she was busy singing with her group and performing at different schools in the neighborhood. Albeit a quintessential shy girl, Pauline's notoriety was on the tip of the tongue of those that like to tap away the nights to the Motown Sound with her tall and slim dark brown brother, Marion, cutting up at the dark and smoky Elks Club downtown.

One thing about Mary Sledge's daughter, Pauline, is that her smile pulled you in almost like bees to honey, a bewitching of sorts. But this time, she was the one that was bewitched by a smile. Her words to me about this guy with so much machismo, "But it was something about his smile," she said; it sent her over the moon. One day after practice with some friends in the band, he, matter-of-fact-like, walked over and expressed that he had a thing for her. And that he thought they should go steady. Now, she felt that she couldn't possibly have a reason to turn away from him because she had been so smitten with him. Pauline didn't hesitate to express to him the rules that Mary and Paul Sledge had established. All Southern Belles can identify this dating rule without a single word being spoken. So as smitten as she was with this guy, he overpowered her after school and sexually assaulted her. Immediately the next day, he shunned her and laughed as he walked in the hallways at school. Shortly after her terrifying experience and the horrid embarrassment, she was doubly embarrassed by her pregnancy as a young girl without a responsible dad or suitor. Eventually, she endured the painful loss of her child.

Terribly, Aunt Pauline expressed this was not the last time that she would be in a compromising situation where a man violated her physical being and emotional security. Unfortunately, later in life, as a grown woman, she endures this horrible experience of sexual assault again. But even at seventy years of age, Pauline continued to have a firm belief in the possibility of a satisfying love with a man. And she was proud to have learned from previous encounters and relationships, and the application of said learned lessons would bode well for her and her next beau. During her visit discussed her current beau and the healthy boundaries she established, and the non-negotiables that she stood firmly behind.

Aunt Pauline learned enough in her life to pass on to a child of her own, and though that was one of her dreams deferred, she chose to take on her nieces and nephews as her extended family and offspring in love. As a mother who experienced infertility, I could relate to her only partly because I could have, keep, and watch my miracle baby grow into an incredibly beautiful person both physically and characteristically. Aunt Pauline was a Phoenix Rising in her way. She sparkled through her courage and zeal for living her best life, finding her only love, in step with her most beautiful music to raise her from the confines of Patterson

Court and West Patton Avenue to a whole new world despite the losses she took early in life with love and legacy.

My chapter on infertility came with a very emotional tax. When Karma was four years of age, her dad and I finally decided to put all of our energy into building our little family from 3 to at least 4. We did all of the family planning steps; going to the doctor to get physicals, looking at our current and future financials to prepare for this family goal. Living in Auburn at the time was perfect for us. We didn't live too far from family, both his hometown and my hometown, and the school system didn't have any bad schools, and I would likely be a future teacher with APS once I graduated with my Master's degree.

Then we heard the echo of my infertility issues again. My doctor reminded me of my PCOS but challenged us with inflamed fallopian tubes. I was devastated and cried in the doctor's office that day. I immediately thought to myself, is this my life? Will I be a woman that struggles with infertility throughout my childbearing years? What did I do to get pregnant with Karma outside of being in love? Fast-forward to our second year after arriving in Alexandria, VA, we reflected on our attempts to expand our family and chose to begin again.

Equipped with prayers from momma, aunts, sorority sisters, and in-laws, we set forth to have another little Cook running around and, more importantly, for Karma to have a young sibling. That February, our little family was flourishing in Alexandria with me at FCPS and Tyree making boss moves with a start-up touring company at the National Harbor, and behold, I had all the signs of pregnancy. The cabinet under the bathroom sink had bundles and bundles of pregnancy tests so that I was prepared to test whenever the signs presented themselves. I joined PCOS communities to learn how to manage my symptoms and encourage my body to be receptive to conception. I was over two weeks late, and I struggled with whether I wanted to tell anyone or even Tyree. I didn't want to jinx it, as they often say. I didn't want to excite him if it was just a false alarm. But I had to tell him, and when I did, we both hugged in excitement. Then he went and told his office I was expecting. And before you knew it, it was a false alarm. This anticipatory event wouldn't be the last time I'd have these hopes, but it was definitely the most traumatic for me.

Eventually, my marriage deteriorated, and that's when I discovered that the sons that I prayed God would give me to give to my ex-husband were given to him by someone else. This news was soul-crushing! A God-fearing woman, traveling every Sunday with my little one in tow to church in Mitchellville, MD. I was replete with anxiety about this news. How could this be when I was the one praying that we'd have a son together. My mother was praying mightily that we'd have another child and, more specifically, that God would bless my womb to produce a son for him (mirroring her own order of children, me then my brother). For months, I was obsessed with the hurtful thoughts of the expansion of his family but devastated by God's answer to my prayer that Karma would be my only offspring. We were left with a divorce and co-parenting efforts.

****

Both my grandmother and my Aunt Pauline are so embedded in my makeup that merely reflecting on their lives gives me the strength to continue accomplishing my goals. So much of them is within me that I am astounded as to the similarities in our personalities and character traits. Aunt Pauline and I shared a sense of fashion, flair, and a love of music. We often talked about this in our long phone calls and whenever we could sit and talk on her visits. When my brother and I went to Texas one summer, we repeatedly bonded over fashion, music, and our flair for life's excitement. I will never forget her courage to live her best life despite the "Ls" she took early in life with sexual assault and infertility.

Me and Ms. Mary bonded over her quest and queries about her little family history and how she continued to make sure that the family she created would never endure the disconnection that Mary had for most of her life. She never really knew her parents, neither her dad nor her mother, which impacted her love and dedication to family. A Davison by DNA, I am a Sledge because of my village. Thankfully, my most recent stop on this journey has me reconnecting with my biological father and the family (aunts, uncles, sister, brother, nieces and nephews, cousins, and all of those in the Davison clan). I didn't have an opportunity to develop rich bonds with them long ago. Although I have walked this earth, connection to my father has been a missing link, a sort of wormhole that never generated the results I searched for along my way. So it was important to me to discover the mysteries of my notable appearance on this earth and ensure my daughter wouldn't walk alone as she goes through life. And as God would have it Karma, has three other siblings to take along on her journey.

Aunt Pauline and I shared a similar reproductive legacy, where mine specifically endured infertility with inflamed fallopian tubes, polycystic ovarian syndrome, and six years of trying to have another child. Aunt Pauline also always emphasized the mandatory requirement for every driver to maintain a road atlas to prevent getting lost. I pray my experiences, along with the lessons learned, are a roadmap for my daughter as she embarks on her journey through life.

 And to mirror my grandmother's experience, my ex-husband's family took me in as their family; we still consider each other family until this day. So although me and Karma's dad are divorced, he and his family are still my *forever-in-love* family because that's how we do it in the South.

So here's to the foundation, my village, and the valuable lessons to chart the course!

Finding Dori...this I know for sure!

I like that

I don't care what I look like, but I feel good

Better than amazing, and better than I could

Told the whole world, I'm the venom and the antidote

Take a different type of girl to keep the whole world afloat

'Cause I'm crazy, and I'm sexy then I'm cool

Little rough around the edges, but I keep it smooth

I'm always left of center, and that's right where I belong

I'm the random minor note you hear in major songs

And I like that

I don't really give a fuck if I was just the only one

Who likes that

I never like to follow, follow all around; the chase is on.

Each year of high school, I received The Most Conscientious Student Award from my violin teacher, Ms. Beth Phillips. Before the monumental transition from elementary school to junior high, my sixth-grade class held a junior high orientation from Carver Senior High School and the Creative and Performing Arts Center. Already a student that stood out from the crowd just due to my reserve and shy nature, I reviewed the listed options for junior high. As I went down the list, specifically inquiring as to which of the options would suit me, I remembered a dream to play the violin and made my selection with pride. So proud of my choice that I couldn't wait to tell my Dad about my newly accepted challenge and discuss all the possibilities.

As a little girl, I was fascinated by the symphony that would appear on the APT channel, the public television station. So before everyone else in the home woke up early one morning, I'd sneak to turn on the floor model television to one of the four channels we had and APT. The symphony was on. I sat squarely in front of this enormous box, just enchanted. Soon enough, my Dad gets up and walks into the front room. He swivels to see what I'm watching on T.V. and says, "Ah, the symphony!" I smile because of the acknowledgment and that I'd found something that I was interested in learning more about it. From then until seventh grade, it was only a dream, but I knew that I'd grab it as soon as I had the opportunity.

Fast forward to seventh grade and the first day of class. My violin teacher had my class first thing in the morning, 9 am, which proved to be perfect in that my fingers nimbly moved on the fingerboard. On this first day, Ms. Phillips introduced herself and a few expectations for the class. She was quiet and kind in her speech and direction. Apricot skin with dark brown flowy curls that swept right under her jawbone, Ms. Phillips was a young European-American teacher, at a predominantly Black high school, with a historic Black name, Black administration, and majority Black teaching staff. Her smile was slightly curved and delicate in that most of her smile was in her eyes and not her cheeks or mouth. The classroom was different from any other class in that it had a hexagonal shape with small rooms off to the side with slender windows—bright white walls with a back wall of windows looking into the courtyard of the school. In the center of the classroom was a small-scaled orchestra set up. There was a side table with some instruments on display; both violins and violas were sitting nicely in their cases. There were also two cellos sitting on their sides on the floor near a music stand. I sat down in the chair next to her, eagerly awaiting my chance to hold the instrument in my hand. Once she went over her introduction to the class, it was time to measure the instrument selected and determine whether the instrument would be on loan from the school or the parent would purchase it. I volunteered myself for the school instrument so that I could take it home immediately.

Once reaching home, I pulled out the instrument and demonstrated my newfound love to my parents. As soon as we arrived home, the phone began to ring; it was Ms. Phillips on the other end. She spoke with them about her observations earlier that day. Ms. Phillips noted that I handled the violin like a natural. She asked if I had had lessons before now. Of course not; it was just the hours of watching others handle the instrument on television. Later, my parents decided to purchase me a violin for as long as I needed, even if I didn't have the same teacher. But for the next seven years of violin class, Saturday orchestra, All-State orchestra competitions, the violin would be my most vested interest. With a first chair designation, constant practice, healthy competition between classmates, volunteer nights at the symphony, and prayer that I'd get a scholarship to college, I'd tout my talent because I was pretty proud of myself for seizing the opportunity and sticking with it for that long. Orchestra was my life from seventh grade to twelfth grade, which meant a busy life that became the fodder for my need for schedules, organization, and a calendar. And because of that devotion to the drill and practice, I'd receive the Most Conscientious Student Award every year.

Conscientiousness- According to the highly-regarded Big 5 personality test, conscientiousness is one of the five traits that can define an individual's personality. People who display conscientious qualities usually work hard and are good team players, making them highly desirable in the workplace.--(Indeed Career Guide, Career Development, Conscientiousness Jan. 21, 2021). In addition, conscientiousness is a personality trait connected with awareness. Conscientious individuals are typically organized, plan their time carefully, and demonstrate self-control.

Individuals considered to be conscientious actively participate in high-quality work professionally and ethically. Often, people who take the initiative require little supervision, dependable, trustworthy, and answerable for their actions. Most often, they set goals and achieve results even in the face of obstacles and competing responsibilities. And last but not least, conscientious individuals strive to get better at what they do and actively seek, accept, and reflect on feedback from others.

See, the award was given to the right student. Those who truly know me can readily co-identify most of these characteristics when they think of me. However, I didn't want this same award, year after year. I wanted some feedback on my efforts over the year, just as the definition listed above. I wondered if she saw me as a most improved student, did she see the results of my additional practice time? I asked if she could see my desire to place for the All-State Orchestra?

Even though we learned that we weren't going or had the funds to go to the competition, I still practiced my music religiously. But every time, I would get the same award. After the first two years, I felt slighted until I received a full scholarship in violin in my senior year of school. This feat proved to be evidence of my hard work in violin class, all while making honor roll, singing in the church and community choir, and my many other activities.

As I began writing this book, I reflected on all the poignant moments of my life that required me to develop a growth mindset. My reflections were revelations about what I hold dear and what matters most, things about life that I know for sure. For the past two years, some of the chapters I'd penned gave me so much anxiety that just considering the chapter brought a full stop to my writing. Going through this process also crystallized what and who was essential and required more of my focus. In the process of reminiscing about my grandmother and the treasures that she left with me as her legacy, I came to realize steps to measure growth, not just the behaviors or characteristics of your work ethic. The concept developed with even more clarity after I willingly became a part of some other villages over the past two years. A series of engagements helped me value my intuition and trust the tools my foundation equipped me with for life's challenges.

This mind shift allows one to take inventory of their growth and glows and how development is maintained. These levels of putting in time and effort, reflecting on the effort given, and embracing the appropriate application of the results compose the concept named Nacr3: Strength, Resilience, and Sparkle! I created this growth mindset formula as a tribute to my southern roots as a Black woman. My grandmother's tenets on life gave me love to strengthen the soul, pearls that will adorn the soul, music to lift our souls, community to support our souls, hard work, and belief in yourself to keep the soul resilient are all we need to be our best selves.

Works Cited

Brown, Brené. *Rising Strong*. Random House, 2017, p. 352.

Maze. *Feel That You're Feelin*. EMI/EMI Records, 29 July 2014.
Featuring Frankie Beverly Live in New Orleans

Monet, Jonelle. *I like That!* Bad Boy Records, 22 Feb. 2018.
Dirty Computer

Noren, Leigh. "How Do You Communicate in a Relationship?"
*Thrive Global: Behavior Change Platform Reducing Employee
Stress and Burnout, Enhancing Performance and Well-Being*, 16
Dec. 2020, http://thriveglobal.com.

Phillips, Lindsey. "American Counseling Association."
Lindseyphillips.com, 1 Apr. 2020, http://Lindseyphillips.com.

Rae, Corrine Bailey. *Green Aphrodisiac*. Virgin, 11 Mar. 2016.
The Heart Speaks in Whispers

Ream, Anne. "GoodTherapy - Find the Right Therapist."
GoodTherapy - Find the Right Therapist, 12 July 2010,
https://www.goodtherapy.org/.

Ross, Diana. *Do You Know Where You're Going To?*
Uni/Motown, 1 Oct. 1975. Theme Song from Mahogany

Scott, Jill. *When I Wake UP*. Blues Babe Records, 26 Apr. 2011.
The Light of the Sun

The Wiz
---. *Soon as I Get Home/Home*. Universal/Motown, 18 Sept.
1978.
The Wiz

Usatynski, Gabrielle. "Couples Counseling & Marriage Counseling in Boulder, CO." *Power Couples Counseling*, Jan. 2014, http://powercouplescounseling.com.

Williams, Pharrell. *Able*. Columbia, 16 Nov. 2016. Hidden Figures

www.ingramcontent.com/pod-product-compliance
Lightning Source LLC
Chambersburg PA
CBHW080404270326
41927CB00015B/3348